To Claire, Malcolm and Claudia

DRINKING IN VOGUE

DRINKING
INVOGUE

Henry McNulty

with drawings by Nigel Paige

ANDRE DEUTSCH

641.87

First published 1978 by
André Deutsch Limited
105 Great Russell Street London WC1

Printed in Great Britain by Ebenezer Baylis and Son Ltd
The Trinity Press, Worcester, and London

ISBN 0 233 97031 2

Contents

Introduction   9
Opening Gambits – Aperitifs   13
Original Gin   19
Whisky or Whiskey?   25
Rum the Sunshine Drink   35
Vodka – it's Vonderful   41
Cognac to put you in Good Spirits   47
The Luxury of Liqueurs   57
The Bold Approach to Sherry Drinking   69
Passionate Port   77
Champagne – Psychological Magic   81
Candy is Dandy but Wine is Divine   91
     White Wines of the World   92
     Toujours Bordeaux   95
     If Not Burgundy . . .   98
     Rosé – Everyone's Best Friend   100
     Wines Around the World   100
     Some Wine Drinks   101
Wine Tasting and Storing   103
A Liquid Form of Summer   111
Some Warming Winter Drinks   119
What's Brewing?   129
Inside Cider   135
How to be Happy but Temperate   141
A Capital Tea   147
Confessions of a Coffee Drinker   153
Index   158

Introduction

My own introduction to alcohol occurred at about age three. Before Sunday services my parson father used to mix the communion wine with water (so as not to lead his flock too far astray and possibly to cut costs). I enjoyed inhaling the delicious vapours that rose from this 'spiritual' preparation. One time, I remember, his church, its belfry infested with bats, was fumigated with huge braziers of sulphur. The yellow glow of the sulphur flickering through the stained glass windows seemed to me a mysterious extension of the aroma of communion wine and made a lasting impression on my infant mind.

Actually, the making of alcohol, though a perfectly natural process, has had quasi-religious associations since the very beginning. It has also long been associated with health and well-being. The medieval alchemists, for instance, believed that wine synthesized the four essential elements of life: earth, air, fire and water. Even St Paul recommended 'a little wine for the stomach's sake', and a modern French doctor, E. A. Maury, claims that it is the best medicine of all. According to this pundit a daily dose of two grammes of alcohol per kilo of body weight constitutes a 'beneficial reserve nutrient' for any healthy person. This is the intake he proposes to those who want to keep both healthy and happy.

In matters of alcohol, as in most things, moderation is the key. In pre-breathalyser days in America, anyone who became immoderate was liable to get into trouble with the law. A tavern keeper could not let a customer 'tipple above the space of half an hour' and had to post the names of those to whom liquor could not be served, in some public place. A man was judged drunk if he 'lisps or falters in his speech by reason of drink, or staggers in his goings'.

As will be apparent, as you read what follows, I like dry spirits: cognac, whisky, rum, vodka, aquavit, gin, and dry white and red wines. But it is a pleasing fact that any alcohol relaxes the nerves and so a judicious quantity will improve most social occasions. It is also beneficial in that moderate drinking at meal times, especially of wine, helps digestion and reduces the risk of an excess of cholesterol in the blood by counteracting the effects of some of the fat inevitably consumed in our modern diet.

Incidentally, as one of the great pleasures in life comes from the use of alcohol in cooking, I have mixed a few food recipes along with those for cocktails, fizzes, punches and the rest. These recipes are not notably low on cholesterol but I think you will find they are high on pleasure. Which brings us to that greatest pleasure of all and the ancient belief in the aphrodisiac qualities of wines and spirits. Listen to Lucullus, an early appreciator of the delights of both meat and drink: 'Take elecampane seeds and flowers, vervaine, berries of mistletoe and dry them in the oven. Crush them into a powder. Give them, in a glass of wine, to the person on whom you have designs and it will work wonders to your advantage!' There are plenty of people still who think along roughly those lines.

In putting this book together I have been deliberately light-hearted for although many weighty tomes have been written on the uses and abuses of alcohol, to me it is purely a source of enjoyment and this I have tried to convey. Though it may be necessary to remind each generation of the perils of excess, the boredom of abstinence and the joys of moderation, I would like to leave you with a few words from Ecclesiastes which perfectly sum up my feelings: 'Wine, measurably drunk and in season, bringeth gladness to the heart, and cheerfulness of mind.'

May it be so with you.

Opening Gambits – Aperitifs

Champagne Cassis, Ouzo with Vermouth,
Dry Manhattan, Pink Gin, Pink Lime,
Red-Hot Aperitif, White Lady, Gin Fizz,
Coffee Cocktail, Side Car,
Hintlesham White Lady, French Kir,
Frappés, Mint Magic

The very idea of an aperitif calls up marvellous mental tableaux to my rapidly deteriorating mind – the harbour at Mikonos, the bar of the Carlton Hotel in Cannes, a terrace at Porto Ercole, boat-race day on Lake Carnegie, flying over Chicago in a tiny biplane.

The word 'aperitif' comes from the Latin, *aperire* – to open – and was originally applied by old-time pharmacists to herbs used as healthy pore openers. My first experience with aperitifs was rather more an eye opener. I had just arrived in Chicago to take on a new job, got in touch with a former university friend, and was instantly ordered to accompany him to the old Chicago airport where some North Shore socialites were holding one of their quaint débutante ceremonials. This one consisted of plying the willing guests with a powerful stimulant or two in the form of dry martinis (one of the best known and earliest forms of the genus aperitif), and then thrusting them, rather less willingly, into small, rickety, open cockpitted aircraft for a loop-the-loop over the Loop. It was a grand and exhilarating introduction to tough old Chicago, which has maintained a soft spot in my heart ever since.

The best of the aperitifs are the simple ones, to my mind. In discussing the aperitif question with a boulevardier friend of mine, not long ago, he opened the conversation with, 'The last time I dined at Lasserre, I impressed my part-time mistress immensely by starting the evening with *Champagne Cassis*. She thought it magnificently ostentatious to ruin the wine of kings with currant juice.' Actually, champagne and cassis suit each other very well, and are a delicious opener to a dinner with wine. You pour only a thimbleful of cassis in the bottom of a wine glass and fill with chilled bubbly. The result is not too sweet, not too strong and pleasingly pink.

Colour, of course, has a potent impact on the senses and helps in the enjoyment of drinks and food alike. Perhaps that is why one of the scenes aperitifs bring to my mind is of a café on the Greek island of Mikonos. As the sun retired behind one of the three hundred or so crenelated, white-washed churches, Costa Gambanis, the unofficial mayor of Mikonos, and I would start our evening meal (well, evening drinking) with a tall glass of ouzo, and delight in watching the clear liquid turn to milky white as we added ice and water, while the town's tame pelican watched approvingly.

Ouzo is only one version of the anise family of aperitifs that you find all around the Mediterranean; called raki or arrack in the Middle East, Pernod or Ricard in France, and plain anis in Spain. If you like the liquorice-ish taste of anise, it is a refreshing sundowner, but it packs a wallop.

All of these anise drinks are distant cousins of absinthe, but without its suicidally depressing ingredient, wormwood. No longer do waiters serve anise, alas, in the old ritualistic way, although I have been served what was supposed to be absinthe in Belgium once, with the traditional slotted spoon over the glass, a lump of sugar in it, and water slowly dripped through it into the 'absinthe' below. It made one feel deliciously decadent. Try ouzo or Pernod with vermouth or in orange or grapefruit juice.

Generally speaking, what the French call aperitif is a bitter tasting affair, despite its sweetness, because of the herbs used to flavour it. Vermouth is probably the best known wine-based aperitif and hundreds of cocktails can be made with it. A *Dry Manhattan,* for example, uses two parts of bourbon, one of dry white vermouth, a twist of lemon, and is served on the rocks or iced and strained.

But vermouth is more than just a liquid to make gin go further. It is a blend of four wines, usually white, but sometimes red, and in France at least, the wine is left outdoors in the sun and rain to mature for a year. Some forty or fifty different herbs and flowers go into its final bouquet, from linden and cinchona bark to forget-me-not and thistle, if the experts are to be believed. The herbed and blended wine is then fortified with a dose of brandy, given six more months in a cask, plus a period of refrigeration, and is ready to drink straight or in your dry martini.

In addition to vermouth, there are many brands of wine aperitifs based on vermouth. There is Byrrh, made of red wine with a touch of brandy and quinine; St Raphael, another quinine-laced red wine drink: and, of course, Dubonnet, a rather bitter-sweet concoction flavoured with Peruvian bark, which – like its colleagues – is best drunk cold, with a slice of lemon, soda and ice. Vermouths such as Cinzano, Punt e Mes, Campari, or Martini and Rossi can be imbibed straight, on the rocks with a twist of lemon (or a twist of orange with Lillet), or as a long drink with soda water added. Cinzano bianco, the white variety, makes a good light summer drink. Italian vermouths are likely to be less dry than French ones. Punt e Mes has been described as 'sweet as a débutante at first sip, but, unlike the débutante, with a bitter [or should it be "better"?] aftertaste'. Chambéry is another distinguished, aromatic, dry vermouth – possibly the champagne of the type.

A 'bitter' vermouth is Fernet-Branca, medicinal to a fault. Some people swear by it as a cure for upset stomachs, for hangovers, and in general, when feeling out of sorts, as an appetizer. There is no doubt that its flavour can shock your gustatory system into awareness, but it is an acquired taste.

You may well prefer cognac taken as a long drink, with water or soda, which also makes a good aperitif. In fact, the British equivalent is often simply scotch and soda or water. By contrast, port is never a starter in England. It is only drunk at the end of a meal. In its native country, however, the Portuguese drink port as a pre-meal pick-up. White port, especially, makes a good introduction to a fish feast. Pre-prandial Lisbon cafés are full of dark-suited men (without women), talking at the tops of their voices so that the only way to get attention to order a drink is by hissing, 'psssst' – a sound that cuts through the cocktail-party noise and reaches even the deafest of waiters.

As a pampered correspondent in Paris at the end of the last war, I, like all newspaper people, was billeted in the Scribe Hotel. The bar was always well attended by such luminaries as Papa Hemingway. But it was a mystery why, since about the only thing they could offer to drink for weeks, was a yellow thing called Suze. Only recently I have discovered one reason for the dismal lack of liquor in those commandeered army hotel bars. The knowledgeable drinkers among the first arrivals in liberated France took good care to sequester as much of the real vermouth, cognac and champagne, not to mention the fine wines, as they could find 'to protect them from the GIs'.

In one of my more impoverished metamorphoses, a well-meaning friend informed me that I could make a fairly reasonable facsimile of champagne by mixing sherry and tonic water. I must warn you, sherry and tonic does *not* taste like vintage champagne. Still, if you are desperate, it can make one more addition to the thousands of things people happily drink to relax with and to enjoy before a meal.

My own favourite aperitif is a glass of dry white wine. That is what I was having in the bar of the Carlton at Cannes when who should slump down beside me but Danielle Darrieux, an encounter not easily forgotten. Actually, although we were introduced, and I offered and she accepted a drink, her interest in me faltered when some handsome film star, probably her husband, took the seat on the other side of her! Still, the wine was good enough to restore my crestfallen ego before too long.

During the war, I was introduced to the British navy's favourite aperitif, Pink Gin. This is another very simple drink and has the advantage of acting like a dry cleaner to your palate. A *Pink Gin* consists of a few drops of angostura bitters, swished around a small wine glass or cocktail glass, a cube or two of ice, and filled up with gin. It is as easy as a martini, and has a lovely pink colour to recommend besides. My first try of it was on the good ship *Umgeni*, honking along in convoy from Liverpool to the Cape. It helped to allay the ever-present fear of 'peril on the deep' but it did not, alas, prevent the *Umgeni* from being torpedoed on her next voyage.

Angostura, because it contained quinine, was originally intended as a malaria cure and was invented in Venezuela by a German doctor. Nowadays it is probably more effective as a cure for hiccoughs, sprinkled on a slice of sugared lemon; and it's made in Trinidad. I like it in a *Pink Lime*, a combination of gin-and-lime and pink gin. Fill a cocktail glass with crushed ice, put in four dashes of bitters and a teaspoonful of Rose's or fresh lime juice. Top up with gin and add a twist of lemon or lime.

In my collegiate spectator rowing days we never called the things we drank on shore, as the shells swished by, 'aperitifs', they were 'cocktails'. But aperitifs they were and their purpose was the same as it is today, to get things going, or to introduce a change in the day's activities. One particular occasion the change was from vernal sunshine outdoors to nocturnal gloom in a speakeasy. And the activity was followed by my first, and large, hangover.

Aperitif drinking varies with national and regional preferences. While the French and Italians possibly lead the field in variety, the Spanish vote for sherry, the Mexicans like tequila, the Scandinavians take aquavit, the Hungarians drink szamorodni, the Greeks ouzo, and so on. There can be individual variation, however, for the vermouth-type aperitif depends on its meld of herbs, and theoretically anyone can make his own by adding alcohol to his favourite 'vegetable'. He'd be lucky if it tastes good enough to drink though, because the blending of the herbs is an art.

The heir of a successful American vermouth maker recalls that his father used to mix up a new combination almost every day and try it out, after it had been 'married' long enough in wine, on his long-suffering family. 'We had a different vermouth every day for years,' the son says, 'and even though my father was a vintner, some of the mixtures were terrible!' One good *Red-Hot*

Aperitif, which you can make yourself, is by steeping red chilli peppers in vodka for a few days. If you like it hot and dry, this will be for you.

Here's a small tip for giving your cocktail or aperitif a jazzier look: add the white of an egg to any and all shaken cocktails. The egg white has no taste, so it does not change the flavour of the drink – but it does make it look nice and fluffy. Everyone knows the *White Lady* (one part of Triple Sec or cointreau, two parts of lemon juice, four to eight parts of gin according to your capacity, and one egg white, all shaken mightily with ice and strained into a glass); and the *Gin Fizz* (two jiggers of gin, the juice of half a lemon, sugar to taste, the white of an egg, and some ice. Shake, strain and pour).

But did you know that an egg white adds a completely new and impressive dimension to a Bloody Mary or a martini or a *Coffee Cocktail* (a cup of black coffee, half a jigger of crème de cacao or cointreau, half a jigger of cognac, and some sugar if you like it very sweet)? In fact, it goes well with a *Side Car*, too (two jiggers of cognac, one of cointreau, a dash of lemon or lime juice, shaved ice), and with any cocktail that needs to be vigorously shaken. And Robert Carrier, the gourmet, in his Hintlesham Hall restaurant has a new version of the *White Lady* which is gin and lemon juice in equal quantities, a dash of cointreau and a touch of sugar to taste, all shaken mightily with the white of an egg and ice, strained and poured.

I mentioned the eyebrow-raising properties of champagne with cassis, but cassis is good with plain white wine, or with white vermouth, as well. The white wine version is called a '*Kir*' in France, after a well-known priest of that name who is supposed to have invented it. All versions are simple. You put half a jigger of the cassis, more or less according to your own taste, in the bottom of a generous wine glass, and fill it up with cold, cold wine or vermouth.

A *frappé* makes a cooling opening gambit to a meal, too. Fill a short glass with crushed ice; pour over it enough aperitif – Pernod, vermouth, Dubonnet, crème de menthe, or what-have-you – to fill the glass up, say a jigger and a half. Sip it through a short straw if you don't like the ice against your lips.

And for romance, what could be more relaxing than a *Mint Magic* as made at the Savoy Bar in London? For a long slinky evening soak a few sprigs of fresh mint in three ounces (75 ml) of white wine for two hours. Add a measure of crème de menthe, four of gin and another three ounces (75 ml) of white wine. Ice, shake, strain and serve with a sprig of mint in the glasses.

PAIGE

Original Gin

Tom Collins, John Collins, Prohibition Cocktail,
Dry Martini, Gibson, Solid Pink Gin, Treetop,
Ramos Fizz, Alexander, Bronx, Gin and Lime,
White Scorpion, Barking Dog, Dog's Nose,
Bulldog, Cat's Eye, Mule's Hind Leg,
Silver Stallion, Elk,
Prairie Chicken, Chantecleer

Having been brought up in the odour of sanctity, so to speak, the offspring of missionaries, my first contact with gin came as quite a shock.

For an innocent schoolboy to go from Greenland's icy mountains and India's coral strand straight into a Prohibition era cocktail party was bad enough. But when the gin was sloshing about in the bathtub – honest – and the host proudly dipped his tumbler into this newly made concoction to toast my arrival, swallowing the whole glassful in one gulp, it made a lasting impression – possibly more on him than on me.

My host was able to give this amazing demonstration because even brand-name gin is simply pure alcohol that has been flavoured with spices, aromatic herbs, and skill. The most ubiquitous of the flavourings used is juniper berries. Early American or bathtub gin was so popular during Prohibition because of this manufacturing simplicity. If you could con your friendly druggist into letting you have some medicinal grain alcohol, you were well on your way to having a potable, if not notable, alcoholic beverage in that by-gone jazz age between the wars.

Original gin, possibly invented by Adam to tempt Eve back, has been around for centuries. The parent of what you and I mix with our vermouth was Holland genever (the word means juniper in Dutch) made by distilling grain spirits and a mash of juniper and things like cassia bark, coriander seed, angelica root, anise, lemon peel, orris root, and other esoteric ingredients. Each maker has his own secret formula. Genever's mash gives it its special taste – so particular that it is really only good straight. If you mix it, it should be with something mild like soda or tonic.

I was grandly introduced to it on that same good ship *Umgeni*, of some forgotten Europe-to-Asia line. Her captain was Dutch and favoured genever, his cargo seemed to be mostly that, plus some 3000 Australian troops being repatriated (the year was 1942), and me, the one American. We happened to cross the equator on July Fourth and the Aussies, ever ready for a party, decided the drinking auguries were auspicious despite danger from subs, and lit into the gin. By nightfall there wasn't a sober breath on board. Even a tiny torpedo would have been devastating for not a soul on the ship could stand up. That taught me what 'Dutch courage' meant!

English gin can be equally stimulating but it is less powerfully perfumed and comes in several varieties. There is the so-called London type, which has much the same ingredients as Holland gin. Some of it is clear as water, some straw-coloured from being matured in oak casks. American gin is similar, though the taste may differ because of the difference in water, used in both to bring down the distilled strength of the spirit to drinkable proof.

Plymouth (brewed in Plymouth) gin has a different flavour from London gins and I believe one of its secret differences is that it omits the lemon peel most other gins use. British naval types are said to drink nothing else in Pink Gin (see page 17) while the original gin sling, the *Tom Collins*, uses Old Tom gin, a slightly sweetened London gin, popular in cold climes. A Tom Collins, (2 oz/50 ml Old Tom gin, the juice of half a lemon and half a tablespoon of powdered sugar) is really, as you will see, a lemonade with gin in it. You shake it well, strain it into a tumbler over ice and add a splash of soda water. For some reason Tom Collinses used to be the thing to drink at tennis parties when I was a lad, but they seem to have dropped from sight since then. Perhaps they are a young man's (or woman's) drink. Worth reviving, though, for they are easy to make and delicious to boot. A *John Collins* is the same formula made with Holland gin. German gin, or steinhager as they call it, has a distinct juniper flavour because it is produced by distilling fermented juniper berries. It often comes in 'stone' bottles. Sloe gin is made by steeping sloe or blackthorn berries in London gin for a couple of months to give it a special taste.

Gin was once the bad boy of the spirits world. Most drinks have a past of some distinction – sherry and the grandees of Spain, rum and the buccaneers, whisky and Scottish lairds in their kilts. But gin became a sort of eighteenth-century tranquillizer, cheap, plentiful and potent; able to take people's minds off the miserable conditions in which most of them lived before the birth of social consciousness in the nineteenth century.

Home production and consumption of gin was promoted as 'patriotic' – a way to use grain so as to help farmers. Taxes on gin were so light that even the poorest people could buy it. You could get 'dead drunk for tuppence' they said, and unlicensed dram shops opened by the thousand. In 1733, in a London much tinier than it is today, there were nearly 7000 of them.

By the time of George II, the grandpa of George III of Boston Tea Party fame, over seven million gallons of gin a year were pouring down British throats. Gin drinking was almost an epidemic and burials outnumbered baptisms by two to one in the London area.

George II's parliament decided to end the uncontrolled sales of gin. Even so, it was still the easiest and cheapest way for the populace to forget its woes. Gradually better education, and better ways of spending free time, combined with the efforts of the Salvation Army and the Blue Ribbon Army (a kind of Alcoholics Anonymous of its day) put an end to these abuses. By the latter part of Victoria's reign gin was becoming acceptable in 'polite society'.

During the jazz age it climbed to complete respectability 'up the stem of the cocktail glass', as a British wine expert once put it. The dry martini is one of the most popular aperitifs in the world, and gin and tonic one of the simplest and most favoured of long drinks. (In Europe by the way, you drop the 'martini' and just ask for a 'dry', unless you want to get a straight vermouth, which, good as it may be, may not be what you thought you ordered.) The fashionable way to make a martini, back in Prohibition days, was to combine one part of French vermouth with two parts of gin and add two dashes of bitters, plus a green olive. Things have definitely changed, and if you are a real stickler for perfection here is the modern ceremonial way to make your *Dry Martini*:

Put a tall pitcher filled with ice into the refrigerator, along with the cocktail glasses. When they are both good and cold, remove them, and the ice. Add a few fresh ice cubes, then four to ten parts of gin, depending on how dry you like it, and one of dry vermouth. Stir quickly and thoroughly. Strain into the glasses. Then, either drink it as it is, or after twisting a sliver of lemon peel over the glass – never, say the connoisseurs, drop the peel in – so the lemon's aromatic oil floats on top. Or you can add an olive.

If you have made more than you need, remove the ice from the jug and keep what's left in the refrigerator till you need it. A *Gibson* is the same thing using a pickled onion instead of the lemon whiff or the olive. And, of course, you can have either of these drinks 'on the rocks', if you so prefer, but that will dilute the original blend.

White Italian vermouth tends to be slightly less dry than French. A real fanatic pours the vermouth over the ice, drains it and then pours the gin on the aromatic ice. A dash of Pernod adds a certain exotic quality to the drink, but then it is no longer a martini.

Gin is actually at its best as it comes straight from the still. Age does nothing to improve it. Its raw materials used to be corn and barley, but now molasses are a major ingredient in its manufacture. Nothing could be more pure, for the best of modern gins are distilled several times, and even today gin is often recommended for medicinal purposes by the family doctor.

Recipes for gin drinks abound. There are gin slings, and rickeys, and collinses and flips and fizzes galore. But I rather like the *Solid Pink Gin*. This consists of flavouring an ordinary quantity of plain gelatine with pink gin. Make the gelatine as the packet tells you to, but replace the water by the same amount of gin, slightly diluted with four or five dashes of angostura bitters. Serve it like a jellied consommé, cold, with half a lemon to squeeze over it. Pistachio ice cream, incidentally, is delicious with gin as a sauce poured over it, and while we are on things green, Angelo, the barman at the Pelicano near Porto Ercole in Italy, makes a cool green *Treetop* with one part gin, one part lemon juice, and three coffeespoons of sugar. Mix with chopped mint leaves and a drop of crème de menthe.

Gin flambés well, too, adding a subtle flavour to fish, for example. When the fish is done (meunière or baked), heat two ounces (50 ml) of gin and pour it over the fish. Then set it alight. Sloe gin flambé gives another distinctive flavour.

There are probably more cocktails made with gin than with any other spirit. A famous one is the *Ramos Fizz*, one of a family of fizzes from the birthplace of jazz, New Orleans. To make this shake two jiggers of gin, an egg white, a jigger of cream, three dashes of orange flower water and the juice of half a lemon vigorously together with some cracked ice. Pour into a tumbler whose edge has been dipped first in lemon juice and powdered sugar. Add soda water judiciously. One advantage of gin is that so many drinks made with it are so easy to concoct. Holland gin stirred in equal parts with St Raphael in a jug with crushed ice and strained into cocktail glasses, for instance. Twist a lemon peel on top. Nicely sour and bitter.

Another simple gin cocktail is the romantic *Alexander*. Two parts of dry gin, one part each crème de cacao and cream, shaken thoroughly with cracked ice and strained into a glass. The *Bronx* is simply three parts dry gin, one part dry vermouth, and the juice of a quarter orange, stirred, strained, and sipped.

Also easy to make is *Gin and Lime* – one part Rose's lime juice and three parts gin, with ice in a tumbler.

For some reason gin drinks seem to remind their inventors of animals, birds and reptiles. One of my favourites in this category is a *White Scorpion*. Maybe it is because I am a Scorpio myself, but I find it delicious, smooth and well integrated. Mix equal parts of gin, vodka, kirschwasser and white crème de menthe with a dash of Rose's lime juice in a shaker with crushed ice. Strain into a wine glass, or pour into a tall glass with the ice. Lovely but lethal.

Other zoological drinks form a sort of Household Pets Section: like the *Barking Dog* which consists of a third each of dry gin, dry vermouth and two dashes of calisay (a Spanish liqueur flavoured with cinchona bark – get it?) and a *Dog's Nose* which is a measure or two of gin in a large glass, filled up with cold beer or stout; or a *Bulldog*, two measures of gin and the juice of an orange in a tall glass, filled up with ginger ale. The cat family is represented by a *Cat's Eye*, or four measures of gin, three of dry vermouth, one each of lemonade, cointreau and water (yes, water) and two teaspoons of kirsch, shaken, strained and served with a lemon twist.

From Down on the Farm come the *Mule's Hind Leg* with a measure each of gin, apple brandy, Benedictine, apricot brandy and golden syrup, stirred together with ice and strained into a glass. Or maybe you'd prefer a *Silver Stallion* – half a gin, half vanilla ice cream, the juice of half a lemon and half a lime (or one whole lemon) shaken with a little shaved ice, strained into a glass and filled with soda water.

The Wild Animal division would surely include an *Elk*, made with half dry gin, half a plum brandy like mirabelle, quetsch or prunelle, and a couple of dashes of dry vermouth shaken and strained into a glass.

The Bird category could include a *Prairie Chicken* – an egg in a wine glass, covered with a measure of gin, salted, peppered and served. Her mate, *Chantecleer*, has two measures of gin, the juice of half a lemon, a tablespoon of raspberry syrup and the white of an egg shaken with ice.

Gin used to be considered an enemy of the working classes, but I am more inclined to agree with the friend of mine who says that work is the enemy of the drinking classes.

Whisky or Whiskey?

Caramel Carrots, Steamed Haggis, Secret,
Highland Cooler, Malt Side Car, Malt Rob Roy,
Dry Rob Roy, Whisky Sour, Palmer,
Rattlesnake, Serpent's Tooth, Crow, Corn Popper,
Old Pepper, Bergamot Tea, Stout Cocktail,
Mint Julep, Cream Punch, Pink Elephant, Kojak,
Irish Fizz, Old Fashioned

It had always been my firm belief that the Scots drink their liquid refreshment either straight or, at the very worst, diluted with a drop or two of 'pure burn water'. On an illusion-shattering trip to Scotland, I found out the Scots will drink scotch with almost anything.

On that occasion my companion, himself a distiller, walked up to the Glasgow bartender and, to my amazement, demanded, 'Whisky and lemonade.' Instead of being thrown out bodily, he was given the mixture without a murmur. I tried it. Actually, it was delicious, but perhaps by then I was slightly under the influence of the several previous nips pressed on me at my friend's distillery.

Heretical as it may seem to the Scots, Scotch whisky is said to have been invented in Ireland and brought to Scotland on an early wave of Irish emigration. Up to that time, the Scots drank brandy like everyone else. The making of whisky has always had something of magic about it and distillers have an almost fanatical aversion to any kind of change in their methods. At one distillery, while barley was being hoisted by rope in a sack up to a loft, the rope broke and the falling sack injured a workman on the ground. Someone suggested using a wire rope in the future but the distiller refused on the grounds that he'd learned his way of making scotch from his grandfather and he wouldn't hear of any substitute that might alter the character of his product!

Real scotch can only be made in Scotland. 'Château-Bottled Scotch' and 'Scotch Bottled at Buckingham Palace' do not exist, Japanese imitations notwithstanding. Even though there are hundreds of castles up there, scotch has humbler origins and most malt distilleries are in small communities hidden in the hills. 'Hidden' because in the early days, a good deal of hanky-panky went on and quantities of illicit whisky found its way down Scottish gullets.

Although it would be difficult to find a true Scot who would admit it, whisky was a very unappreciated drink until about a hundred years ago. Up to that time the chic drink had been brandy. But a microscopic and unwelcome American import – in the form of a horrid little bug by the name of Phylloxera – changed all that. Somehow, Phylloxera made the trip to Europe, where, from 1863 and for thirty years thereafter, it devastated the vineyards, sinking its snout among the roots of the vines, sucking out the sap and leaving them to die. (For some reason American vines had been immune to attack.) Since brandy is made from wine, and less and less wine was available for brandy distillation, supplies of that fashionable drink became short. The élite began to turn to scotch. By the time someone discovered that European grape vines could be grafted onto immune American roots, thus foiling the pest, someone else had found that a blended whisky cut down the strong peaty taste of the straight malts the Scots loved and that the resulting beverage could be sold to delighted foreigners.

Scotch has never looked back. Before the vine-pest, Scotland made about 16 million gallons of whisky. By 1897 it was making 31 million gallons. Today it is producing over 150 million. So, in a way, Americans can take some of the credit for the success of scotch.

In another way, so can the French, for it was French brandy that was supplanted, and the French themselves are today great supporters of scotch (they drink $4\frac{1}{2}$ million gallons of it per year), although this is a comparatively new development, dating from the second world war. I can remember a French New Year's Eve party, just after the war, when scotch was first appearing on the scene in Paris. My hosts did not really know what it was, nor how to drink it. We were served the stuff in tumblers, filled to the top as if it were wine or water. Most of the guests did not last until midnight.

Scotch lovers will go to great lengths to enjoy their favourite tipple, especially when it is in short supply. One whole regiment of Canadians of my acquaintance got into trouble for using a bit too much initiative during the war while suffering from ennui and thirst in some forsaken part of Scotland, where there were more distilleries than guards. They obtained a gooseneck awl from the supply depot and snaked this through a warehouse window to drill a hole in one of the storage vats within. With a length of hose, they then siphoned out enough gallons of fairly raw, but ageing, whisky to render the whole regiment less than useful in case of an emergency, such as an invasion.

Back in England in 1905 there was a famous law case known as the 'What is Whisky?' case. The pure one hundred per cent 'single', malt whisky distillers – malt whisky being virtually the original scotch – were upset that their brew was being cut with grain whisky to make its strong taste more palatable to the unreconstructed British. The blenders won, and the blend is legally scotch, but opinion is still divided in Scotland as to whether it is really.

Malt whisky is one of the four basic types of ingredients the Scots believe must be part of any good blend. Since blending is done by smell rather than taste, a blender is known as a 'nose'. You should have, the 'noses' say, an island malt, a highland malt, a lowland malt, and a grain whisky in every bottle of fine drinking scotch. Considering the fact that a quality blend has sixty-five different whiskies in it, you could hardly miss having some of all the four essentials in any good brand you would be likely to buy.

Once I was marooned on the island of Islay for eight hours because the one and only plane that flew me to the single malts needed attention. One of my travelling companions found the place so enchanting or possibly intoxicating that he bought himself a house there during those few hours. He has spent all his vacation time there ever since, near a huge peat bog. The very bog that belongs to Laphroaig, one of the most aromatic of the single malts. Divine to its fans (its flavour has been described as 'a mixture of seaweed and tarry rope'), this unique and marvellous delicacy owes its special flavour to the smoke from chunks of peat, carved out of the neighbouring soil with huge wooden spades and piled along the roads to dry before being used for malting.

I was once given a little known malt whisky recipe for carrots that comes out slightly caramelly, and tastes superb: slice up one and a half pounds (675 g) of carrots and put them into a pan, raw. Mix in a tablespoon each of lemon juice and sugar, two tablespoons each of butter and your favourite malt whisky, and a little salt. Stir this around with the carrots over a low flame until the butter melts. Cover and put in a medium hot oven for an hour, stirring once in a while.

The business about 'light' scotch often puzzles the Scots themselves, for the amount of alcohol in the drink is the same whether the drinkers call it light or heavy. To the real aficionado, the only true scotch is the 'single' malt whisky – that is, one that comes from a single distillery and is made exclusively from malt. Most people would consider this fairly 'heavy', I suppose, because of its pronounced peatiness. From that extreme, through blending with the other types of whisky, especially grain whisky, the taste of the pure malt is subdued until you get what the American whisky fancier likes, at the other end of the spectrum which has a higher percentage of grain whisky. Some Scots complain that some of these very 'light' types are not scotch at all.

There are over one hundred distilleries making malt whisky and more than a dozen grain distilleries, and the number of brands is legion – something like five hundred in Scotland. If you can stand up to it, you can try them all on a Saturday night in Glasgow.

A mountainous whisky salesman once made me try almost all of them on a pub crawl in London. This two-hundred pound, six-foot-six giant was determined to show me up as a frail and backboneless imbiber. We began the tour at ten in the morning, and because whisky salesmen believe eating is a waste of time, we went straight through scotch after scotch until seven in the evening without a bite – avoiding the statutory closing hours by spending those empty stretches in private clubs where there are no such restrictions. By sticking strictly to scotch and water I managed to arrive home still on my feet, to the astonishment of my huge friend, and the concern, to put it mildly, of my wife.

A favourite dish of mine to go with malt whisky is haggis, that old Scottish joke. But don't laugh, at least not until you've tried it. It is a gourmet treat when well made – like a spicy sausage. Traditionally, the Scots use a sheep's stomach to wrap the sausage in for boiling, but this isn't necessary. Any big sausage casing will do or you can put the ingredients in a bowl and steam them instead. Here is how: boil half a pound (225 g) of liver (calf, sheep or pig) for forty minutes, and cool in the broth. Mince the liver finely and pass it through a sieve. Parboil two onions and chop small. Chop half a pound (225 g) of beef suet. Put a cup of Quaker Oats in a thick, dry pan and toss them over a flame until brown. Add the liver, onions, suet and season with salt, pepper and cayenne. Now add mixed Italian herbs – marjoram, thyme, oregano, basil, rosemary, savoury and sage, or any combination thereof that you like. Moisten with the broth until it is sloppy. Turn into a greased bowl and steam for two hours. When you dish up, serve tots of straight malt whisky, or pour some over the haggis itself. This may not be the traditional recipe, which calls for the inclusion of chopped sheep's hearts and lungs and boiling rather than steaming, but it is a lot simpler and very good.

If you are one of those whose morale depends on a little something in a balloon glass after dinner and want to taste what whisky must have been like in the good old days, you should try one of the great single malts. The best include Glenlivet (the oldest obtainable being twenty years old), Glen Grant, Glenfiddich (ten years old), Talisker, Glen Flaggler (eight years), Glendullan (twelve years) and dozens more. Scattered among the mountains and islands of Scotland they may have near neighbours whose products are not at all of the same quality – much like the variation of wines from different vineyards in France.

The Park Avenue or Mayfair of the whisky making area of Scotland is an area of about 900 square miles on the River Spey, one of the world's best salmon fishing rivers. Near by is the Scottish skiing area of the Cairngorm mountains, and some lovely seaside golf courses at Lossiemouth and Nairn. Some of the local inhabitants think the healthy quality of the air in the region is due to the three million gallons or so of evaporated scotch suspended in it and thus supposed to be 'lost' each year. These fumes, from the kegs where the whisky is ageing, are a form of pollution many of us would like more of.

Now for a few business notes. Malt whisky is almost as interesting as an investment as it is a drink, but with 115 malt distilleries in Scotland what they make is by no means a production-line commodity. Prices vary wildly like grain futures, so whisky buying is speculative in the extreme. There is no organized Whisky Exchange, no official list of buying or selling prices, and no guarantee that a parcel of whisky will produce profits. In short, the best formula for a would-be whisky investor is to trust his nose, count costs, and take a few risks. For those of you who like something more solid for your money there is always the possibility of becoming a distiller. In Scotland anyone can do so simply by applying for a licence, which costs about a pound. There are, however, a couple of small hitches, like having to build premises that the excise authorities approve, and the plant has to be of commercial size. But still (oops, sorry), it's a lovely dream.

Until recently, much of the Scottish whisky drunk around the world was aged in American barrels. This was because American whiskey regulations insisted their distillations should only be aged in new kegs. The result was they shipped their once-used kegs, still in excellent shape, over to Scotland (and sometimes even to Spain, for sherry) to be used again.

Despite this co-operation, the two whiskies are in fierce competition for the American market, different though they are in taste. The American version is fermented in two ways: sour mash and sweet mash. Sour mash used for bourbon, simply indicates that the mash from a previous fermentation goes into the new batch of yeast and mash, and makes the fermentation period last longer. Used for rye and other American whiskies, sweet mash is fresh yeast entirely, and fermentation is faster.

Bourbon, by the way, did not get its name from some royal Spanish or French connection, but because the Pennsylvania emigrants who took off for Kentucky and the Wild West to make their fortunes, and some new distillations, from corn (maize) instead of from the traditional rye, decided to name the new stuff after their new home – Bourbon County. Today nearly three quarters of all American whiskey comes out of Kentucky stills.

So many Irish poteen-makers infiltrated the American scene as refugees from the potato famines a century ago that, as you may have noticed, America uses the Irish spelling with an 'e', instead of the Scottish without. Irish whiskey is made mainly from barley and is distilled in pot stills like scotch. It tastes different from scotch because the malt used is not dried out over peat fires, and it is usually aged for longer before being drunk.

Canadian whisky (they use the Scottish spelling) is a blend of corn, rye, barley and wheat. It is a light alcohol, more like American whiskey and very slightly sweeter perhaps. It is extremely popular even in the United States.

Other countries make whisky – notably the Japanese whose distillations are remarkably good. If you are a visitor to that land, they are the only whiskies you can buy without going broke. Even Spain has tried to make 'scotch', so far with little success, but perhaps one day their methods will improve.

Apart from scotch and soda, or water to taste, and the lemonade mixture described on page 26, there are many ways to entertain with scotch. One I like is the *Secret* – a measure of scotch, three dashes of crème de menthe, ice and soda. Or try a *Highland Cooler* on a hot summer day – a measure of scotch, the juice of half a lemon, two dashes of bitters, sugar to taste, then fill with ginger ale and ice.

Or a *Malt Side Car*: two parts malt whisky, one part cointreau, one part lemon juice. Shake, strain, and serve. While a *Malt Rob Roy* goes something like this: two parts of ten-year-old Glenfiddich single, one of sweet vermouth, a dash of bitters, ice. Stir and strain into a glass. This Rob Roy has a pungent, subtly different flavour.

To make a *Dry Manhattan* the up-to-date barman uses five parts of bourbon to one of dry vermouth and a dash of angostura, stirred with ice (made with scotch, this same mixture becomes a *Dry Rob Roy*). He'll make a *Whisky Sour* with one part sugar syrup, two parts lemon juice and eight parts bourbon or rye – sometimes scotch or Irish whiskey is used instead of bourbon or rye but the smoky taste of scotch is never ideal with citrus juices. If you prefer your Whisky Sour without sugar then it becomes a *Palmer*

The reptile world is well represented among whisky drinks: a *Rattlesnake* uses eight measures of rye whisky, two of lemon juice sweetened to taste, three dashes of Pernod and the whites of two eggs. Rattle very hard with ice, to make it nice and fluffy, and strain into glasses. Shakespeare said that a thankless child was sharper than a serpent's tooth, but this *Serpent's Tooth* cocktail might have changed his mind. Fairly sharp, it consists of two parts of Irish whiskey, four of dry vermouth, two of lemon juice, one of kummel and a dash of angostura. Stir and strain. If you prefer a high-flyer try a *Crow*; two-thirds whisky, one-third lemon juice and a dash of grenadine.

A *Corn Popper* makes a good punch: a pint of bourbon, a cup of cream, two egg whites and a tablespoon of grenadine. Shake without ice then put into glasses with an ice cube and fill with soda. Or for a really sensational drink try *Old Pepper*, the pepper being Tabasco. This one will really knock your head off for it consists of a dash of Tabasco, two dashes of angostura, a teaspoon each of chilli and Worcestershire sauces and a measure or two of whisky. This volcanic mixture is shaken with ice (which it surely needs) before pouring.

Leave it to the French, however, to come up with something new – a whisky drink blending the moribund idea of cocktails with their newest experiments in food, la Nouvelle Cuisine. Why not, say the *enfants terribles* of modern French cooking, critics Gault and Millau (their magazine *Le Nouveau Guide* covers the food, wine, and travel scene in France and their restaurant and hotel guide is a competitor to the Guide Michelin), mix in a shaker a measure of tea flavoured as the Russians do with bergamot, half a measure of a light scotch, a dash of vanilla essence and a drop of angostura? This you serve in a tall glass with ice, filled with mango or passion fruit juice. Or, if you find that a bit too 'nouvelle', how about equal parts of iced tea, champagne and bourbon – another of their suggestions? Mr Gault and Mr Millau admit they are being a trifle adventurous in proposing such things, but they think it's time to demolish some of the ancient monuments of cocktaildom. Imagine, for instance, a tall glass filled in equal quantities in the sequence that follows, with scotch, cold sweet Sauternes and Guinness stout!

If you don't know a *Mint Julep*, there is something missing in your life.

You have to marinate fresh, dry mint in five tablespoons of whisky per serving for an hour. Crush some ice to powder and fill a tumbler with it. Add two teaspoons of simple syrup (made by mixing two parts of sugar to one of water, brought to a boil and cooked – it keeps forever refrigerated), and stir. Add mint, fill with bourbon. Stir once more and stick in a sprig of mint. Perfectionists make each glass separately. Some insist on a silver mug, but I like to see my drinks, and prefer a tall glass.

Cream Punch is nourishing. Pour a jigger of bourbon, quarter of a cup of single cream and a dash of vanilla into a shaker with a teaspoon of powdered sugar and some ice. Shake thoroughly, strain into a tumbler and sprinkle the top with nutmeg. This is nice and relaxing after a hard winter's day.

The London Hilton concocts a *Pink Elephant* by mingling a jigger of bourbon, the juice of a lemon and three dashes of grenadine. These are shaken hard with ice and the white of an egg and served in a martini glass. Users of the Hilton's 007 Bar also like a Kojak, probably because it is tough and smooth. A *Kojak* has that same jigger of bourbon with an ounce (25 ml) of passion fruit, a dash of dark rum, and half an ounce (15 ml) of pineapple juice, shaken and served over crushed ice in a wine glass – with a lollipop, of course, as a muddler.

Irish whiskey blends agreeably with curaçao in an *Irish Fizz* – two measures of Irish whiskey, a teaspoon of curaçao, a bit of sugar if you think the curaçao not sweet enough, and the juice of half a lemon. Shake with ice, strain and fill the glass with soda water.

One of the best cocktails as far as I am concerned is a ceremony in itself – the *Old Fashioned* – which should be lovingly and carefully made with a base of American rye whiskey, though you can make it with scotch. You need a small, heavy-bottomed tumbler or two to put it in. First drop in each glass a lump of sugar, and sprinkle it with a few drops of angostura bitters. Melt the lump with another few drops of water. The resultant pink mess is spread around the sides of the glass with a spoon. Only then pour in a measure or two of whiskey; stir, drop in two cubes of ice, add a slice of lemon and half a slice of orange, a maraschino cherry if you like, and a squirt of soda.

I told you the Scots would drink anything as long as there is scotch in it!

Rum
the Sunshine Drink

Rum Punch, Punch-à-Crème,
Sorrel Liquor, Mona's Rum Punch, Modern Grog,
Daiquiri, Marie Galante, Port Royal, MJP,
Planter's Punch, Cuba Libre, Black Rose,
Rum Cow, Fishhouse Punch, Rum Pot

You may think of rum as an occasional fun-drink, something to give a party extra swing, but that would be because you've never been to the Caribbean where the real thing is made and rum is more a way of life.

According to my friend Mona Defour, an amber-skinned Trinidadian beauty who is a reliable source of knowledge on this subject, rum is used for an astonishing variety of things from seasoning meat, especially 'the wild game that is found in the forests', to soaking dried fruits in the preparation of Christmas and wedding cakes. It seems that it also 'improves the flavour of freshly made orange and grapefruit juice', which isn't surprising, though one might never have guessed at yet another use – as a sort of precursor to Johnson's Baby Cream it was often mixed with coconut oil and smoothed on bathtime babies to keep them soft and rash free.

But let us get back to rum for fun for, as one might have expected, it turns out to be one of the most adaptable – blendable and mixable – of the alcoholic drinks.

Rum is a spirit distilled either from sugar cane juice, in the old-fashioned way, or from molasses. The United States is the world's largest producer of rum from 'blackstrap'. In Colonial days, rum was used as ballast when ships returned empty to Europe after a slave trip westward and Moravian missionaries shared space in the old 'rum and Bible ships', as they sailed to Labrador for preachments, with these more mundane spirits at the turn of the century.

Rum is made wherever sugar grows, even the Russians make some. But the Caribbean is its true home where some of it is as smooth as silk. In the islands most people drink it almost as soon as it comes out of the still. But it is probably preferable to wait for a blender, a sort of spirituous adviser, to marry the various types and give you a legitimately wedded and properly mature blend. This takes about three years, but rum continues to improve in oak casks for twenty years or more.

Almost wholly confined to sailors in its early days, rum drinking became popular during the cocktail era after the First World War. Rum's flavour depends on the esters (or impurities) in it, and there are almost as many flavours as there are islands in the Caribbean. Rums tend to be darker and heavier the farther south you get. Jamaican and Martiniquais rums are the most highly flavoured, with two or three times as much esters as the US made stuff and five times as much as the light Cuban version.

Some Jamaican rum is like a black syrup it is so thick, while Barilla rum from Puerto Rico is almost as clear as gin. Guyana Demerara has things like plums, raisins, and spice added to give it a fruity taste. Pale gold Cuban rum is hard to find these days. Barbados rums are often flavoured with bitter almonds, sherry and even raw steak!

Old New England was once a big rum-producing area, and the tax on rum was one of the irritants that led to the Boston Tea Party and the Birth of a Nation. In fact, Paul Revere is said to have stopped for a tot of rum before setting off on his famous ride – whether to bolster his courage or to keep warm is a moot point.

Rum is what makes the Caribbean world go round, and the national drink, no matter what nation you may visit is *Rum Punch*, slightly varying from place to place, but basically similar. The Trinidadian version is made by mixing one bottle of dark rum with syrup – made with one and a half pounds (675 g) of cane sugar in one quart (1·1 l) of water, boiled until the sugar dissolves – the juice of eight limes, and several dashes of angostura bitters. Stir well and serve with crushed ice and a cherry. Sprinkle each drink with ginger or nutmeg. The longer it's kept the better it becomes, so make a lot and keep it cold.

Another version is *Punch-à-Crème*. This takes six egg yolks beaten into two tins of evaporated milk and one tin of condensed milk (depending on how rich and sweet you like it), until the mixture is thick and creamy. Into this pour half a bottle of dark rum, add several dashes of angostura, sprinkle the drinks with nutmeg and enjoy.

The way to drink this and every other rum mixture, according to Mona, is to pour the amount you can drink into a glass, open your mouth, let the liquid slip slowly down your throat and swallow immediately. You can chase it with water or a soft drink but, unlike whisky, it is not to be mixed with water or ice and is definitely not a drink to be sipped.

The strongest rum drink in Mona's lexicon is a perilous potion, commonly known as TDL (Trinidad Dangerous Liquor), and only very strong people can drink it. Other favourites are Old Oak, Black Label, White Star, and Vat 19, and a very popular one that comes from Barbados called Mount Gay Eclipse. But even the local population finds these tough to drink straight and apparently a lot of the older people still make their own smooth blend with coconut water which was the only soft drink to hand when they were young.

Mona's own invention is a rum liquor made with sorrel. Make a tisane by pouring boiling water on half a pound (225 g) of sorrel flowers, from which the petals have been removed. Let this cool, strain and sweeten to taste. Mix one pint (6 dl) of this infusion with one pint (6 dl) of rum and let it stand for five days. Drink it then, neat, as an after-dinner liqueur. Another good liqueur-like concoction is made with coconut, green ones preferably, but 'up North' dry, brown ones will do. Bash in one of the eyes, pour out the milk and fill the nut with young rum. The white type is best for this. Plug the hole and leave it for six months – the longer the mellower – in a cool place. Some even bury it in the ground for this ageing period. Then drink it neat.

Mona Defour claims that rum punches improve with age, so she makes up large batches and keeps them refrigerated. Her punch, which can be heated by thrusting a red-hot poker into the brew (better use a metal drinking vessel if you do), needs a bottle of dark rum, syrup made with one and a half pounds (675 g) of sugar dissolved by boiling a quart (1·1 l) of water, the juice of eight limes and several dashes of angostura bitters. Serve in tall glasses and sprinkle each separate drink with ginger or nutmeg.

The British are great connoisseurs of rum, perhaps because their naval tradition decreed that sailors should have a tot of rum before going into battles, of which they used to fight a wearisome number. Grog, of course, was a much-used heating device three hundred years ago, originally spiked and spiced with gunpowder. It was Samuel Pepys who signed the order, as Secretary of the Admiralty, that allowed rum to be issued to ships' crews instead of brandy. But a *Modern Grog* has little affinity with Admiral Vernon's original 'quart of water to half pint of rum'. Today you use one part each of rum, cognac and strong tea, add a small glass of curaçao, mix and pour into a large glass until it is half full. Fill with hot water, sugar to taste, and add slices of lemon.

In St Michael's Alley, not far from the Bank of England, is one of London's oldest 'cauphe houses', the Old Jamaica Wine House. Founded by a Turk named Pasqua Rosee, according to an old 1795 guidebook the 'best rum is obtained there', and Rose's Jamaica Rum, Lemon Hart, Captain Morgan, Coruba and Myers rums are still specialities of the house. A nip or two of these nectars prepares you admirably for an excellent meal at the George and

Vulture, an almost equally ancient, noisy and crowded pub across the street.

Most rum drinks are sweet because sugar or sweet liqueur is often part of their recipe, but you can experiment with leaving out most or all of the sugar. A *Daiquiri*, for instance, is two ounces (50 ml) of Baccardi rum, a teaspoon of sugar syrup and the juice of one lime, shaken and poured over crushed ice. A *Marie Galante* is three parts Martinique rum, two Triple Sec, and the juice of one lime. A *Port Royal* uses one part Jamaican rum, one part Tia Maria, one teaspoon of lime. This is supposed to cause the bells of a sunken church off Port Royal to peal at each ministration.

Try an *MJP* for a dry rum drink. This is a jigger of dark rum, the juice of half a pink grapefruit, no sugar, lots of ice. Stir and drink.

Planter's Punch is a lime drink best with fresh limes, but Rose's will do. A tot of this goes in a cocktail shaker mixed (if fresh lime is used) with two tea-spoons of sugar. Add two measures of rum, then soda or water and ice to your taste. Shake and serve very cold in tall glasses.

A *Cuba Libre* is ideal for freeing that romantic feeling: it's the juice of half a lemon and a tot of rum with cracked ice in a highball glass that is then filled with coke. In a black mood, a *Black Rose* might cool and cure you. This takes ice in a tall glass, a teaspoon of sugar, a tot of rum and cold black coffee.

A *Rum Cow* needs a measure of dark rum, two drops of vanilla extract, a pinch of nutmeg, a dash of angostura, two teaspoons of sugar and a cup of milk, all shaken well with ice and strained into a tall glass, while a *Fishhouse Punch* is the thing for a small party. Dissolve three-quarters of a pound (350 g) of sugar in a large punch bowl with water. When completely dissolved add a quart (1·1 l) of lemon juice, two bottles of Jamaica Rum, peach brandy to taste, two quarts (2·2 l) of water, stir. Put a large block of ice in the bowl and chill the mixture for an hour or two. These quantities should do for a party of about twenty-five people.

And finally, there is *Rum Pot*, an old German idea that can be both imbibed and ingested. Fill a large container, that can be tightly closed, with layers of sliced fruit – bananas, pineapple and orange are good together or plums, cherries and apples – pour in enough rum to cover the fruit and let it stand for a week or more. The liquor becomes very fruity and makes delicious sipping, while the fruit itself is marvellous on ice cream.

The sky looks different here

PAIGE

Vodka –
it's Vonderful

Abdug, Coffee Vodka, Lemon Vodka, Tarragon Vodka,
Pink Vodka, Vodkatinis, Russo-Spanish Cocktail,
Franco-Russian Cocktail, Green Treetop,
Grand Gimlet, Screwdriver, Bathtub Vodka,
Bloody Mary, Bob's Bloody Mary, Bullshot,
Bloodshot, Moscow Mule, Red Lips, Cooch Behar,
White Shoulders, Black Cossack, Rasputin

A Russian will never drink vodka by himself. The reason is that, to drink at all, protocol demands he propose a toast. How to do this if you are alone? So there must be a companion to whom to make your little speech. Only then are you allowed to throw your tiny ice-cold glassful down your parched throat – in one gulp, of course.

Given the companion, and toasts being absolutely essential, the next problem is the toast itself. Russians will cook up almost any excuse to offer one – to home and country, to racing, to the president, to a pun, to love. A Russian friend of mine knew a man who lived alone but always came home needing a drink. This desperate and wily Russian solved the 'You can't drink alone' problem by catching an earwig. He tied it to a long thread. When the earwig took off, he had his excuse for the Bon Voyage toast. When he pulled the bug back, 'TAM!' time for the welcome home toast. The man lived happily ever after, she says.

There is no need for us, not being Russian, to be quite so formal about it, since vodka is a beverage for which it is easy to find all sorts of uses. It has no taste in its pristine form, and no smell, so it will mix with anything. For instance, in Iran where some of the best vodka is made, they have a deliciously refreshing summer drink called *Abdug*. You mix about equal quantities of club soda and plain yoghurt in a tumbler, adding spearmint if you fancy the taste, and a jigger of vodka. Top it off with a pinch of salt.

In the only Russian restaurant in Teheran, vodka is served spectacularly encased in ice. You can make this idea yours by putting the spirit into a small carafe holding about half a bottle. Place the carafe in a tin large enough to hold it plus enough water to surround the carafe. The whole lot goes into the freezer. When the water is frozen, submerge the tin in hot water for a moment, slide the iced bottle out, and what you get at the table is a handsome block of ice surrounding the vodka, which is at just the right temperature for imbibing.

Of course, this icy treat is drunk with caviar, and possibly because both the vodka and the caviar are said to be aphrodisiac, the combination enjoys an enormous success in success-minded, exotic Persia. In almost equally glamorous Paris, near the not-so-exotic, but famous, former Paris *Herald* offices on the rue de Berri, there is a sort of Aladdin's cave presided over by a French genie who takes an ounce of caviar every morning for his breakfast with a nip of vodka. The caviar is easy for him to get because his cave is the storehouse for all the caviar shipped from Iran to Europe for distribution. The breakfast, he claims, is the secret of his health and energy, for he says it 'has more vitamins than most foods, and is rich in lecithin, which fortifies the nervous system'.

The medical kick reminds me of a young British doctor who, using twenty willing volunteer drinkers at the Middlesex Hospital and testing different types of alcoholic beverage, came to the conclusion that vodka produces the least painful morning-after side effects of any spirit. Possibly this is because vodka is very 'pure'. It is distilled twice and filtered through charcoal to rid it of any unwanted taste or smell and the best of it is cut with distilled water.

As a matter of fact, the very word 'vodka' seems to have a psychologically suggestive effect at times. Vodka, in Russia, means 'little water'. A member of the Georgian princely family, Tschavtschavadze, who lives in Paris, told me that his grandfather was once promised a marvellous aged vodka just before going off on a hunting expedition. The beverage was lovingly and reverently handed to him as he sat on his horse before taking off. He tossed it back in true Russian style and fell off his horse with shock and chagrin. The 'marvellous aged vodka' was nothing but 'a little' water. The disappointment nearly killed the old man.

And it's an old Russian custom to make a young bridegroom undergo a pleasant form of torture before he marries. On the wedding table in tiny vodka glasses, the name of his bride is spelled out. He must polish off all these before he is allowed to take her. Unfortunate if her name is Anastasia.

Actually, the Russians and Poles drink their vodka with such light-hearted speed because they are afraid of becoming drunk on the fumes. They claim that by sipping you inhale more alcohol than you drink. They like it 'with a tear' – that is the outside of the glass frosty with cold. And they like it coloured and flavoured. And why not? They do this at home by putting various herbs into the original flavourless vodka. Saffron makes it yellow, sunflower seeds give a mauve tint, cornflowers turn it blue and walnut shells brown.

As to taste, you can vary that too, to suit your mood. You can have a vodka tasting with vodkas you make at home. There is rowan berry, cherry, honey or red pepper – to name a few. Russian vodka used to be made from potatoes. Now most of it is made from grain, but it can all be flavoured. My favourite is the Polish version of zubrovka (the Russians make this too), which contains a slip of the herb of that name, a grass on which the European bison feeds, it seems. This gives it a nutty taste and a slightly green tinge.

You can make vodkas with flavours from coffee to lemon, or to your own formula. For a *Coffee Vodka* you need four cups each of sugar, water and vodka and half a pound (225 g) of freshly ground coffee. Pour one cup of vodka over the raw grounds and let sit for a week. Make sugar and water into syrup and add to it rest of vodka. Then combine coffee vodka with syrup vodka, strain, bottle and store six months to let all blend smoothly. Depending on your intestinal fortitude, you then drink or sip.

For *Lemon Vodka* you grate the rind of three lemons (or you can use two oranges instead, if you'd rather have an orange taste). This you cover with vodka and allow to stand for four days or so. Make a syrup of two cups each of water and sugar, strain the rind out of the vodka, pour both the lemony vodka and the rest of bottle (about four cups) into the syrup while still hot. Strain the whole thing again, bottle, and store at least a month. *Tarragon Vodka* is easier still – you just put some fresh tarragon into the bottle and let it sit for a week or two. Red pepper, of course, not only makes a good hot drink, but comes out satisfyingly pink as well.

Kingsley Amis, the literary drinker, has a marvellous idea, which he applies to vodka's cousin, gin, but which is equally useful with vodka. The stunt is always to have a small bottle of angostura at hand because with that and the vodka you can 'knock together some sort of drink' under almost any conditions. For instance, a quickie *Pink Vodka* is three drops of angostura, swirled around in a glass, ice, vodka and away. W. H. Auden, a poetic imbiber, apparently had a fairly regular schedule in that 'at ten to six I start on the vodka martinis'. I don't know his formula but *Vodkatinis* consist of five to eighteen parts of vodka and one of dry vermouth, depending on your passion for dryness.

If you have Spanish blood, or no vermouth around the house, try a *Russo-Spanish Cocktail* – a Vodkatini with dry sherry instead of vermouth. And to be really wild, make a *Franco-Russian Cocktail* with vodka and a drop of Pernod.

If you have an eye for green, there is a nice line in green concoctions: a *Green Treetop* consists of one part vodka, one part lemon juice, a teaspoon of sugar more or less and some ice, mixed in a mixer with chopped mint leaves and a drop of crème de menthe. Pour into a tall glass and top with soda water. Looks like, and almost convinces you that you are in, a tropical lagoon.

Any brown-eyed beauty might become green-eyed with interest over a *Grand Gimlet* served as a long drink and consisting of four parts vodka, one part Rose's lime juice, ice, soda water and a sliver of fresh lime.

Vodka does not clash with wine. If you start with vodka, switch to wine during a meal, and go back to vodka, you can still hold your head high the next morning. That British doctor with his hangover tests says that a mixture of pure alcohol and orange juice is the most clear-headed alcoholic thing to drink – the ingredients of a *Screwdriver*. Anyone can make this famous beverage which was supposedly invented by American oil-rig workmen and so named because they stirred the concoction with screwdrivers.

In Paris a few years ago, opposite the Caviarteria, on the Boulevard Latour-Maubourg, I got the gastronomic shock of my life. Two hard-hatted, blue-jeaned French workmen pulled caviar and a tot of vodka out of their pail and munched for lunch this food of kings before whacking in the next rivet.

Paris is a great vodka City, perhaps because so many White Russians invaded it after the First World War as taxi drivers. They not only drank it, they found it stimulating for rubdowns after a hard day fighting traffic.

One beautiful Russian lady had a huge success with her own brand, bottled and labelled with a very official-looking Russian double eagle, and sold in the fanciest restaurants in Paris. What she did not tell her customers was that she made it at home in the bathtub. If you want the recipe, here it is: take a pint of pure grain alcohol and mix it with a pint of distilled water in which you have dissolved half a lump of sugar. Bring this nearly to the boil, light a match over it, and let it burn for five seconds, covering it immediately. Cut the peel of one lemon into a bottle and pour the mixture into it. Shake vigorously so the peel permeates the liquid. Cool it and refrigerate for a week. Filter lemon out, and you have a fine 'home-made' vodka ready for mixing.

Everyone has his own recipe for a *Bloody Mary*, perhaps the most popular vodka drink of all, but the most usual one consists of one part vodka to about six parts tomato juice. To this you add Worcestershire sauce, Tabasco, or any other unsweetened spice. Sometimes a little lemon juice is mixed in, and often freshly ground pepper and some salt as well. If you make your Bloody Mary in a blender, you can add celery leaves and the white of one egg, so that you have a sort of vegetable salad pick-me-up all in one go.

Robert Carrier, gourmet and restaurateur, makes a Bloody Mary with the usual one measure of vodka to two measures of tomato juice but with half a measure of lemon juice, celery salt, pepper, a dash of Tabasco and then another dash or two of sherry which, says Bob, 'glues the flavours together'. He then shakes all this energetically with ice until it is a foamy, frothy, aerated pink delight and ready to drink.

Another good combination of food and drink is a *Bullshot* – especially as made by Tony, the bartender at the Berkeley Hotel's Perroquet Restaurant in London. His version consists of a tumbler of beef bouillon – any good tinned bouillon will do – a measure of vodka, salt, pepper and a dash of Worcestershire sauce. The whole is tossed in a shaker and served on the rocks. A seafood version is made with clam juice instead of beef bouillon.

Or even a *Bloodshot* – a measure each of vodka, tomato juice and tinned consommé plus the juice of half a lemon and a dash of Worcestershire sauce, served on the rocks. A *Moscow Mule* uses the juice of half a lime, which you drop with the rind into a tall glass. Fill with ice, add about two ounces (50 ml) of vodka and top up with ginger beer. Stir.

You might like to try the invention called *Red Lips*. It consists of a measure of Campari, half a measure of vodka, three measures of grapefruit juice, ice and a decorative mint sprig or two. Soda water to top it up if you want.

A strictly adult beverage with a guaranteed built-in glow – not to say bushfire – is a thing called *Cooch Behar* after the Indian maharajah of the same name. Although it was invented in India, the drink adapts beautifully to cold weather. This individual central heating system is made by steeping one of those red-hot Mexican or Italian peppers in a bottle of vodka. The longer you leave it, the hotter the liquid gets. Then the 'improved' vodka is added to tomato juice and the whole served on the rocks.

Other exotic drinks are: *White Shoulders* – a jigger of vodka, half a jigger of curaçao, and one of double cream, mixed in a blender and served in a large glass over ice. *Black Cossack* – that jigger of vodka in a tall glass filled with cold Guinness. *Rasputin* – a jigger of vodka in tall glass with ice, fill with clam juice, stir, add olive with anchovy stuffing.

The Russians tell a joke about recruiting for their army. The new boy is asked if he smokes. 'Yes.' 'Then you must stop.' If he likes women. 'Yes.' 'Then you must stop.' If he drinks vodka. 'Yes.' 'Then you must stop.' 'Will you die for your country?' 'Sure. What else is there left to live for?'

Cognac to put you in Good Spirits

Italian Manhattan, Arco-Iris, Sol y Sombra,
Brandy Sling, Brandy Scaffa, Orchid, Almond Blossom,
Spanish Rosita, American Rose,
Cheese and Brandy Dip, Brandy Mayonnaise,
Brandy Vinaigrette, Brandy Balls, Brandied Duck,
Lobster au Cognac, Brandied Fruit

The gathering was glittery, the guest list distinguished and well stocked with French titles and names from the newspaper and publishing worlds, the setting superb. The scene was the mansion of one of the big cognac families. Not only was the best plate out, but the food and wines – not to mention the brandy – were fabulous.

As the gloved waiters poured the wines they would lean over and murmur into each guest's ear the name and vintage of the wine. 'Beychevelle '43,' they would whisper. 'Grands Echezeaux '45,' or 'Yquem '34'. Finally an American journalist who had not stinted himself could stand it no longer. He staggered to his feet, raised his glass to the astonished French assemblage, and cried, 'Rutgers '36'.

The Americans laughed. The French, of course, did not get the joke – he was quoting the name of his university and the date of his graduation there-from – but the Cognacais with their long history of civilized behaviour, took it in good humour and the journalist was not ridden out of town on a pole. Possibly he got away with it because about the only gourmet invention, apart from brandy itself, to come from Cognac is a rather strange device for allowing you to eat more – the *trou du milieu* or 'hole in the middle'. This consists of taking a small glass of straight cognac between the third and fourth courses of an eight-course dinner to clear the throat and generally stimulate your gastric juices to greater effort.

One of the nicest things about the town of Cognac is that the air is heavy with the delicious smell of evaporating brandy. One brandy producer, who came to France from Sweden, used to say that this had forced him to give up his morning exercises. When he threw open his bedroom windows and took a deep breath of that brandy-laden air, he became so intoxicated he couldn't work for the rest of the day.

This phenomenon does not seem to worry most of the local inhabitants, however, for the Cognac region has the highest proportion of gaffers over one hundred years old in the whole of France. To a man (and to a woman) they attribute their longevity to either drinking in or breathing in the local product. They may well be trying to keep up with the reputation of their brew, for though there is no such thing as true Napoleon brandy, it can be very old, and the process of making even the three-star variety is a long and meticulous one.

Only brandy from the Charente region of France is legitimately cognac. This area lies in the west, not far from La Rochelle. The wine from the Charente vineyards is so acid it is practically undrinkable as wine, but it distils superbly, a process handled mainly by the farmers themselves – some eight thousand of them. Because the small farmers do not have enough storage space, the spirit is then sent to the big shipping houses like Courvoisier, Hine, Martell, Hennessy, Remy Martin, and Bisquit Dubouché, to name but a few, for blending and ageing.

The shippers age the spirit in oak kegs stored in huge warehouses. During the war, it was easy for the German occupiers to detect hidden stores of cognac, for the evaporating fumes from these kegs seem to make the perfect atmosphere for a certain kind of black roof fungus. All the authorities had to do to spot a cache of cognac was to climb to a high point and pick out the black roofs!

Brandy does not go on ageing for ever. Some experts say it reaches its prime at about forty years. Most of what we drink is between four and twelve years old. The wine is distilled in burnished, onion-shaped copper stills. Once distilling starts it must be kept up continuously, day and night, until the whole supply of wine has become brandy. This means that the workmen must sleep on the job to keep the boilers burning and the wine flowing into the stills. They camp on beds right in the distillery, sometimes for several weeks, while their fond wives keep them supplied with food and bottles of vin ordinaire. Their transistor radios provide the only other entertainment.

Newly-made cognac is white and is poured into huge vats to blend. It is then transferred into the kegs that are to hold it for the next four or five years or more as it matures. A good deal is lost from each keg through evaporation as the liquid seeps through the wood, but though the makers deplore this loss, it is a necessary part of the process that turns firewater into a smooth after-dinner drink.

Once bottled, brandy ceases to age, so don't be fooled by a cobwebby bottle into thinking it must be old. All those stars and letters on the labels likewise do not necessarily indicate age. In case you don't already know it, the V stands for very, the O for old, the S for superior, and the P for pale. The rest of the lettering system is as easy to work out: F for fine, X for extra, C for cognac – what else, indeed?

4

Since cognacs are a blend, and since every famous producer tries to maintain the same character in his cognac each year, the way to decide which brand you prefer is to experiment until you find the taste you like best at the price you want to pay. The Remy Martin version is dark and caramelly; Courvoisier's is sharper, while Camus, Hine, Martell, Otard and Monnet are each distinguished in their own way. Because it should average ten to twelve years of age, VSOP is the best buy in terms of value for money.

Cognac estates are sometimes run on rather baronial lines. I was once being guided through the vineyards of a famous house by the proprietor when he suddenly decided he wanted a pair of secateurs. He clapped his hands, and like magic, five flunkies appeared out of nowhere and dashed up to find out what the old man wanted. Reminded me of medieval times.

The estates can be very beautiful. One time we were wandering along the River Charente with the photographer Gjon Mili en route from a distillery photo session to dinner, when we noticed he had stopped behind. Oblivious to us, to hunger, to anything but the beauty of that exquisite scene he was taking a picture of a small pool, half covered with fallen leaves. He got to dinner about an hour late.

The dictionary says brandy is alcoholic liquor distilled from wine or fruit juice and this covers a multitude of pleasures – from Armagnac and similar brandies to marc and white eaux de vie.

Brandy itself is a good autumn drink, perfect for sipping by an open fire and, if you are a smoker, excellent as a cigar dip – wet the mouth end of the cigar with brandy before you light it. Its name is shortened from the Dutch, *brande wijn,* and as seems to happen when words transfer from one language to another (as with the French with *un dry* for a dry Martini, or *le self* for a self-service restaurant) its English version retains only the least important of the two words, *brande,* which just means burnt.

Armagnac is a much smaller brandy-producing region – the land of the Three Musketeers – with a mystique of its own. A really old Armagnac can cost fifty pounds a bottle and up, but ten-year-olds can be found for much less. Most of them are made by small private stills – no big names like cognac. Try to ensure that the word 'Bas-Armagnac', appears on the label. And buy those that are made and sold by the proprietor. Some good names are Samalens, Sempé, Marquis de Montesquieu, Marquis de Puységur.

Apple brandy from Normandy, calvados, is another good autumnal beverage. Drinking young calvados is like swallowing a nutmeg grater, but a properly aged one, say fifteen years old, is an after-dinner delight. In the States this kind of brandy is called applejack. We used to make our own by letting cider harden, then freezing it with a straw in the centre of the block. The alcohol, which remained liquid, could be poured off through the straw to become apple brandy.

Spanish and Portuguese brandies taste sweeter than the French, with more flavour of the wood in which they are stored. They are 'comfortable' drinks with a pleasant bouquet. Which reminds me of a disaster that befell me during the war, after an eight-hour flight from Lisbon to Bristol in a blacked-out KLM Dakota. I was carrying two bottles of the Lusitanian brew in my coat, which was slung over my arm. Just as I entered the customs shed at Bristol airport, one fell out on to the cement floor, breaking and spreading a wonderful but embarrassing perfume throughout the building. The customs men were most sympathetic and at least as sad as I was.

Cyprus, South Africa and Australia also make brandies that have their own characters and flavours. California is another producer. American brandy is clean and light. German brandy or 'brantwein' is often made from French grapes imported from Cognac. As a result Asbach Uralt is as similar to cognac as any 'foreign' brand can be. Italy has the sweetish, grapey Stock brandy and claims to produce fifty million bottles of the spirit yearly. They even – the Mafia is everywhere – push an *Italian Manhattan*: equal parts Stock-84 and red vermouth with a cherry. Brandy distilled from the must of grapes, that is the skins after the wine has been pressed from them, is made in France as marc and in Italy as grappa. Sometimes rather fiery and raw, both can be excellent if properly aged in the wood. They are good served cold.

There are a host of other brandies made from fruit. The latest craze in France is a red spirit made from raspberries. This is used like cassis, a teaspoonful or so in the bottom of a glass, with cold white wine poured over it, to make a Kir-like drink. This version is being promoted by the Nouvelle Cuisine brigade and is delectable.

The more traditional white framboise and its cousins, poire William (from pears), kirsch (from cherries) and mirabelle (from those small, absolutely delicious yellow plums) are all dry brandies, joyous drinking cold, or sprinkled over fruit, or as a flavouring for ice cream.

Brandy makes a good mixer, as well as being good straight. A Portuguese idea is an *Arco-Iris* (rainbow to you) which is equal parts of crème de cacao, crème de violettes, yellow Chartreuse, maraschino, green Chartreuse or Izarra, and brandy. Each should float on the other layers, so pour carefully and slowly. A *Sol y Sombra* is easier – half cointreau, half brandy. A *Brandy Sling* uses a dash of angostura bitters, the juice of a lemon, sugar to taste and two measures of brandy. Fill with plain water, ice cubes, and stir. And if you are in a sweetish mood, a *Brandy Scaffa*, served unchilled and undiluted, is made with that same dash of angostura, then equal parts of maraschino and brandy.

Brandy and flowers seem to go well together: the *Orchid* uses half a measure of cognac, one and a half measures of gin, half a measure of crème de violettes and half a teaspoon of lemon juice and one egg white. Shake them all up with ice, strain and add five or six drops of crème de violettes. Float a flower on top, an orchid preferably. The *Almond Blossom* is one and a half measures of cognac, one of gin, a teaspoon of lemon and half a measure of orgeat almond syrup. The *Spanish Rosita* can be as rosy as you please, depending on the amount of grenadine you use. Basically it is one part each apple brandy and dry French vermouth, three parts gin, grenadine to taste or to colour, shake with ice, strain into a glass, add a twist of lemon peel and a cherry for extra pinkness.

The *American Rose*, oddly enough, is made with French ingredients, possibly owing to the literary invasion of Paris between the wars by expatriate American writers like Hemingway. It uses a measure of cognac, a dash of Pernod, a teaspoon of grenadine and two slices of crushed ripe peach. Shake with crushed ice, strain into a large wine glass and top up with champagne.

Most people think of brandy as something good to drink, but it should also be thought of as an adjunct to your shelf of herbs, condiments and flavouring. It is the cook's best spirit, a little of which goes a long way.

Choose the brandy to be used in a particular dish by the effect you want to create. If you want a dry wallop of a taste, then a young three-star brandy is right. If you are after a full, gutsy flavour, an Armagnac would be the thing to use. For delicate sauces, made with cream, a smooth old cognac blends nicely. When you are flaming a dish, an inexpensive brandy from Italy, Spain or Germany will do since you are then only interested in the flavour that remains after the alcohol is burned off.

You can use brandy straight, slightly warmed, heated, or entirely flamed away, again depending on what taste you want to end up with. In an egg-nog, for instance, brandy should be used uncooked, and the same goes for the hard sauces made with butter and sugar to go with puddings. In stews or sautéed dishes you can use the brandy either warmed or flamed. In the first case, the alcohol evaporates; in the second, it burns up, and you will have to try the two methods for yourself to see what the difference is in taste. In both cases however, it is the residual flavours that count, and they are delicious.

Flaming food is not just a gimmick carried out in restaurants to impress you; the flames do eliminate extra fat. Coq au Vin, for instance, gains by having the ingredients ignited. This eliminates the greasiness of the sauce, and makes the dish supremely digestible.

As a quick guide, here are some of the ways to use brandy in food. (In most cases I am prejudiced in favour of cognac, but this is a matter of personal taste – any brandy will give you the same kind of results.) Starting with starters, cognac blended with cream cheese or blue cheese and chopped nuts makes an easy, tasty dip. A drop or two in lobster bisque, onion soup or consommé is heady and delicious. Lobster thermidor, of course, requires it. Use it straight in creamy sauces for fish, shellfish, and mushrooms, when reducing them. Flambé braised chicken, beef, lamb or game so as to burn off excess fat and add an exotic flavour. For steak sauce, add straight cognac to pan juices. And, of course, adding brandy makes an ordinary pudding into a festive one. For instance, you can soak the apples in it before you make apple pie and dampen sponge cake or macaroons with it. You can also sprinkle a little over vanilla ice cream.

For something more unusual you might like to try some of the following recipes which can be made with cognac or any other brandy. Take *Brandy Mayonnaise*, for instance. In this you simply add a teaspoon of dry white wine, a teaspoon of brandy, and a tablespoon of whipped cream to a cup of your basic mayonnaise (which can even be of the bottled variety if you are in dire straits). The same can be done with vinaigrette sauce. To one cup of this you add a jigger of brandy and a teaspoon of tarragon. This will make any salad taste marvellous.

A beloved aunt of mine gave me an old American recipe for *Brandy Balls* that you might like as a different kind of sweet. This requires two cups of crushed plain biscuits, one cup of finely chopped pecans or walnuts, two tablespoons of melted butter, two of light corn syrup, two of cocoa (or you can use chocolate biscuits instead of plain and omit the cocoa), a third of a cup of brandy, and one cup of powdered sugar. You mix all the ingredients and form them into large marble-sized balls. Roll them in powdered sugar or crushed nuts after they are formed. Now cover them and store them for a week to allow the flavours to meld nicely before enjoying them.

There is also *Brandied Duck* for your delectation. You will need two ducks, salt and freshly ground pepper, half cup cognac, one cup dry red wine, two large onions, chopped, one tablespoon chopped parsley, half teaspoon thyme, half teaspoon marjoram, quarter teaspoon allspice, one bay leaf, one table spoon butter, six tablespoons olive oil, one clove garlic, crushed, and half a pound (225 g) mushrooms, sliced. Cut up the ducks and marinate them in a bowl with a mixture of salt, pepper, brandy, wine, onions and herbs for at least four hours, turning the pieces now and then. Put the butter, oil and garlic in a heavy frying pan and when hot, add the marinated duck. Brown the pieces well, then add the mushrooms and strained marinade. Cover and simmer for about an hour and a half. Remove the duck to a hot platter, thicken the sauce by quick boiling and pour it over the duck.

More ideas? Add brandy to taste to chicken liver pâté. Veal kidneys, properly cleaned, sautéed, and flamed in brandy are one of the gastronomic treats of the world. Flambé pork chops or veal escalopes by simply pouring a jigger of brandy over them in the pan, and lighting it. *Lobster au Cognac* is easy to do. A two-pound lobster, four tablespoons of butter, a pinch of dry mustard, some thyme, salt and freshly ground pepper, and six tablespoons of cognac are all you need. You split the lobster, or have this done for you, and clean it. Put it in a baking pan, shell down. Mix the butter, mustard and thyme and spread on each half with salt and pepper to taste. Stick in a medium hot oven for fifteen minutes or more, basting well. Put on a hot platter, pour the liquid over, add cognac and light. Baste again, and serve.

Brandied Fruit are the easiest of all preserves. You simply get the nicest fresh peaches, cherries or apricots you can find, prick them thoroughly with a skewer or knitting needle to let out the juice, and put them in a wide-mouthed jar. Cover them with cognac, adding sugar if you like (about a teaspoon to a big peach), and cover so the air doesn't get inside. Then let stand for three or four months. This makes a delicious dessert, eaten with cream if you want to be really piggish.

To get back to drinking, let me end with a suggestion about glasses when you drink a good brandy straight. Those huge balloon glasses that sommeliers love are not the best. They concentrate the fumes too strongly, and are worse than ever when the glass has been artificially heated. A small, tulip-shaped stemmed glass, warmed by the hand that holds it, is probably the best way to enjoy both the aroma and the taste of a fine cognac. 'Santé!'

The Luxury of Liqueurs

Wallbanger, Heering Fizz,
Scandinavian Cherry Dip, Black Russian,
Café Calypso, Chartreuse Mix, Alexander's Sister,
Grasshopper, Green Izarra Jelly, Green Dragon,
Green Eyed Monster, Marnissimo,
Home-made Peach Liqueur,
Sorbet aux Framboises, Chinese Herb Highball,
Angostura Ice Cubes, Hippocras, Green Beret Basque,
Rose Water, Danish Mary

An untimely breach between me and my bride at the very start of our married career was avoided by the soothing intervention of a liqueur. We had decided on the Costa Brava for our honeymoon. The only trouble was my boss dreamed up a super crisis at just that moment which brought him to visit me in Paris. So I had to stay behind while my wife took off on our honeymoon on her own.

Fortunately she found there a great and good friend who had the genius to introduce her, and eventually me when the crisis passed, to what I still think is the greatest of after-dinner liqueurs – crème de menthe. Poured over crushed ice, it is the most refreshing mouth-reviving drink I know. And it did a lot to smooth over a temporarily somewhat strained family relationship. I can still see that hornet-waisted bottle (those bottles) of Gets Peppermint sitting on our honeymoon balcony as we sipped and waited for the sun to sink slowly across Palamos Bay. (Actually, it was a long wait. The bay faced east, but by then we didn't notice.)

Liqueurs offer a huge range of tastes, from fruit and flower flavours, to anise and walnut; from very sweet to the driest of dry. They can delight the eye with a variety of colours, and best of all, they make a delicious and gracious finish to a meal. They are made in many ways – by distilling, by macerating, or by mixing essential oils with spirits, mainly brandy and grain alcohol.

After-dinner drinking is a universal relaxant. The Chinese after-meal beverage is rice wine with which are associated many longstanding traditions. At a feast guests used to be met by a sort of Master of Ceremonies who bowed to each one and led him to the host. After more bowing, the host went to the empty chair where the guest was to sit, pretended to dust it, and raised the guest's cup of wine in a toast. The guest bowed; the host bowed and returned to his own seat. Both bowed again and sat down. Nice and slow and relaxing. The Chinese, by the way, are said to have produced a spirit called alaki from rice wine as far back as 800 BC, so they have had time to develop the ceremonial approach to the after-dinner drink.

As after-dinner drinks, liqueurs have been popular in the West for centuries. A novel, if messy, way to take liqueurs was practised a hundred years or so ago at the Duke of Mecklenburg-Strelitz's court. The Earl of Effingham, a guest, would sit opposite Lady Effingham at dinner and feed liqueur chocolates to her by throwing them across the table into her mouth, to the vast amusement of the duke's friends.

France produces hundreds of different liqueurs, but Italy manages to produce a few score, too. Probably the best known are Strega, with a taste like Chartreuse, made from a mixture of seventy or more herbs, and Galliano, which claims to be the top-selling liqueur in the States. Galliano is alliteratively purified through 'fossil filters' and converts an ordinary Screwdriver (half orange juice, half vodka) into a *Wallbanger* if you splash a bit of it on top.

Getting to know what you like for producing that after-dinner sigh of relief is part of the game of becoming a connoisseur and no connoisseur will ever be an alcoholic because for him alcohol is only one element in a composite work of art. There is such a tremendous variety of after-dinner drinks to select from that the art of selection is doubly therapeutic. It not only relaxes you, it allows you to exercise your own judgement and maintain your individuality in this day of mass-produced, supermarket conformity.

A liqueur with a deliciously dry finish is Cherry Heering, an invention of the daring Danes. Its dryness comes from using fresh cherries plus the crushed cherry stones in the distilling, which gives the final product a subtle almond taste. Usually this is an after-dinner drink, either on or off the rocks. but a *Heering Fizz* can be a pre-meal delight too. It needs one tablespoon of granulated sugar dissolved in a little water, the juice of half a lemon, an ounce (25 ml) of cognac and the same of Cherry Heering all mixed with cracked ice and served with a lemon slice.

In Scandinavia they mix cream cheese with cherry brandy to make a dip, or to spread a cucumber withal. You cut the vegetable in half lengthwise, dig out the seeds, and fill the hollow with the spread. Chill it in the refrigerator and slice into bite-sized chunks.

Another unusual liqueur is made with coffee (only the most aristocratic beans of course), and comes from Jamaica. This is Tia Maria, of which one measure mixed with one of vodka and served over ice becomes a *Black Russian*. Or, in proportions of three-quarters of a measure of Tia and half a measure of dark rum, in a cup of black coffee, on which floats a layer of cream, you have a *Café Calypso*.

Benedictine was first brewed in 1510 at Fécamp Abbey in France. A monk dreamed up the formula for his new cure-all, found it made his colleagues feel better if they were tired or sick, so he called it D.O.M. still used on the label and standing for the Latin, *Deo Optimo Maximo*, 'To God, most good, most great'. Now, made by a family-owned firm in Fécamp, only three people are supposed to know its formula.

Chartreuse, another monkish brew, with a brandy base and herbs to give it taste, comes in two versions – yellow at 86 proof, and green at 110. Naturally it has an affinity with brandy. It has had a chequered career since it was invented in 1607. Made by an order of silent monks near Grenoble in France, it first ran into trouble during the French Revolution when its secret formula was commandeered by the government. The civil servants of the time could not understand the monkly notations about the one hundred and thirty herbs in its recipe so, fortunately, they gave the papers back without destroying them. The liqueur was banished to Spain in 1903 because the Order itself was expelled from France, but the monks went on making it in Tarragona. In 1940 production was once more allowed in France and today it is the only liqueur still being made by a religious order.

A good long drink with Chartreuse requires the juice of a lemon, a teaspoon of sugar, a measure of cognac and a couple of dashes of Chartreuse, shaken with ice, strained and topped with soda water. Something like Chartreuse, Green Izarra, the best liqueur of the Basque country in south-west France, is good too, and equally delicious frappéed. Both can be served solid in the form of jelly dessert simply using the liqueur for flavouring. Add half a cup of liqueur to each cup of jelly, in the normal way, instead of some other liquid, and serve ice cold with cream.

For eight people, try a frozen *Alexander's Sister*: put half a cup of crème de menthe, the same amount of double cream, two cups of cognac or gin and four cups of ice into a blender. Blend and serve in stemmed glasses.

Crème de menthe is used to produce the greenness in some of the most interesting drinks in the lexicon of the bartender. Like the *Grasshopper* – one ounce (25 ml) each of crème de menthe, crème de cacao, and single cream, with half a cup of crushed ice, shaken vigorously, or whirled in a blender, and served in stemmed glasses.

There are at least three different recipes for another green drink, the *Green Dragon*. The first dragon for slaughter is made by stirring together two ounces (50 ml) of vodka, three-quarters of an ounce (20 ml) of crème de menthe and some ice, then straining the result into a glass. The second mingles equal parts of green Chartreuse and cognac with ice. Stir then serve. The third dragon needs one ounce (25 ml) of crème de menthe, one and a half ounces (40 ml) of gin, half an ounce of lemon juice, four dashes of peach bitters to be shaken with the ice then strained into a glass. All three of these recipes are for one serving.

Having conquered the dragons, the *Green Eyed Monster* remains for your vorpal blade to snicker snack. This consists of equal parts green Chartreuse, gin and vermouth. (The original recipe calls for sweet vermouth, but not having a sweet tooth, I prefer to use dry.)

Grand Marnier has a special association for me with Le Mans because of the thin, thin crêpes I had there flavoured with it, and the *Marnissimo* that, after a miserable stand-up meal of croque-monsieur, as the cars roared round the course, made such a lovely dessert. For a Marnissimo put a teaspoonful of powdered sugar in a wine glass, add two measures of heated Grand Marnier, fill with hot coffee and stir. Float half an inch of whipped cream on top and serve, taking care not to disturb the cream until your first sip.

There are liqueurs made from a base of fruit, beans or kernels and others which get their flavour from herbs, flowers, leaves and blossoms. They can all be used in cocktails, or as after-dinner drinks, in a variety of ways: with cream or eggs to make them smooth, with brandy, gin or whisky to cut their sweetness, with lemon or lime juice to add tartness.

Some liqueurs that go well with coffee are the less cloying flavours, like Drambuie, Strega and Anisette, but even the extremely sweet ones can be tempered by mixing them with brandy. Brandy itself, as a long drink, is another favourite – what the French call a fine à l'eau – brandy, water, ice.

The 'white' fruit liqueurs are probably the driest of all. The most ubiquitous type is made from plums and is called variously mirabelle, slivovitz, quetsch or pflumli depending on where you happen to be in Europe.

Other fruit is turned into lovely liqueur brandies for after-dinner drinking too. Raspberries give us framboise, cherries turn into kirsch, and one of my favoured after-dinner drinks is Williamine, or Williams, made by the Swiss and French out of William pears. This blends extraordinarily well with fresh pineapple, incidentally. All the white liqueurs are strong, with luscious fruity aroma, and leave a pleasant essence-of-fruit taste in the mouth.

You can even manufacture liqueurs yourself by steeping fruit and herbs in grain spirit with a little sugar – the precise proportion of fruit or herbs in commercial varieties is seldom disclosed but you can always experiment and peach brandy is a good thing to start with.

Peel enough peaches to fill a large jar, or several jars. Cover them with sugar and close the jars loosely with lids. Keep on sugaring the peaches until the juice is drawn from them and the sugar dissolves. Once they are covered with their own juice, tighten the lids, wrap the jars in heavy paper and put them in a cool, dark place for three months. You can then use the peach slices on ice cream, while the liquid is poured off and bottled. This makes a delicious liqueur just as it is but you can also add cognac to it if you like.

Liqueurs are nearly as good in solid form as they are to drink. By that I mean they make delicious condiments in, on or over food. Fruit-based liqueurs, for instance, go well with the fruit they were made from: apples soaked in calvados, strawberries in fraises, cherries in kirsch, or prunes in mirabelle, accent tastes with delectable decadence and pleasing authenticity.

Other liqueurs are ideal as sauce for ice cream. Calvados is marvellous flamed with game, or unflamed and mixed with your favourite pâté. Roast duck basted with kirsch is not bad either. In the pudding department, green Chartreuse whipped in cream and poured on grape salad, makes a good start. Then you can graduate to the sweet soufflé with Grand Marnier, and the chocolate cake made with Kahlua in the batter.

Sorbet aux Framboises for twelve people uses one and three-quarter pints (1 l) of sugar syrup to which you add and mix the juice of two lemons, and seven and a half ounces (215 g) of pulped raspberries. Put this into an ice cream freezer and spin. When almost set add one egg white whipped stiff. Put in the deep-freeze until set, when it is ready to serve. Over each serving pour a handful of raspberries and three tablespoons of framboise liqueur. Drambuie whipped in cream and poured over strawberries also makes a fine finish to a meal.

Quality after-dinner liqueurs are made with natural ingredients. Some houses even blend them specially for VIP customers. One such was King Edward VII. King's Ginger Liqueur was made for him by Berry Bros & Rudd, that 'ancient and authoritative source of wine lore' whose shop in St James's Street in London has hardly changed in one hundred and fifty years. The King's doctor asked BB&R if it 'could produce something warming for His

Majesty to take after his winter morning's drive in his new motor car'. BB&R could and the result successfully did the trick. Its spicy ginger flavour is still an excellent stimulant on a cold night after a grand dinner. A similar pepper-upper is Leroux's Ginger Flavoured Brandy.

Every now and then, even today, I can be whisked back both in time and space to China and my childhood by certain smells. One that does it is a whiff of super-low-octane petrol, probably mixed with oil, that immediately calls up a picture of the old boat-bowed Renault taxis in Shanghai as they pooped and polluted their way down Bubbling Well Road. Another is the hot fragrance of sesame-seed cakes which reminds me of those we bought from street ovens to feed the huge golden carp in the S-Ts-Ling gardens in my 'home town'.

The aroma of spice triggered a fantastic coincidence in my life and led me to a recipe for a drink of distinction. A regular London typhoon had forced me and two hundred others to shelter in one of the city's delightful shopping arcades where I stopped by a small Indian shop. An attractive brunette was talking to the Hindu shopkeeper and tasting his spices. I overheard her say that the fragrance reminded her of her infancy. Her family frowned on children eating 'native' food from street vendors, she said. My family did too, and I interrupted to say so. 'Oh,' says the beauty, 'where were you born then?' 'China,' says I. 'Me, too,' says she. 'Where in China?' 'Soochow,' I replied. 'So was I,' says she. 'And what's your name?' I told her and her eyes popped. 'You know, I think your father signed my birth certificate!'

We lunched a few days later, and she was right. There on a document belonging to a lady I'd never seen before in my life, was my father's spidery writing – and out of seven million Londoners, 12,000 miles from where we both started.

At our rather convivial repast she told me about a herb drink that I shall now pass on to you. It needs a mixture of herbs that may ferment before use, but since fermentation improves it, you can't lose. But beware of explosions! Mix six sprigs of chopped fresh mint and the same of borage with half a cup of lemon juice, the zest of one lemon and a teaspoon each of unchopped borage and lemon balm. Allow to stand for at least two days. Using a highball glass, put in ice, a dash of angostura, a dash of the herb decoction (it will keep), a slice of lemon, a measure of cognac, and top up with tonic or ginger ale.

After those China days, I graduated to more sophisticated fragrances. Take that amalgam of aromatic herbs and spices, angostura bitters. It is to certain cocktails of gin, rum, brandy and bourbon what salt is to food. Tony, the bartender at the Berkeley Hotel in London, has a novel way of using it. He warms a dry ice tray, sprinkles a quarter teaspoon of angostura into it, and sets it alight. Then he fills the tray with water and makes ice cubes, pink and inviting, for vodka and gin drinks.

An unrivalled stimulant, according to Norman Douglas, the author of *South Wind*, is a *Hippocras*, which means a wine highly flavoured with spices. His recipe consists of a bottle of Burgundy, an ounce (25 g) of crushed cinnamon, two pounds (900 g) of icing sugar, one ounce (25 g) of ginger, and a quarter ounce (7 g) each of cloves and vanilla. Mr Douglas is not very informative about what to do next, but I imagine it is steeped for a week, the bottle tightly corked, then drunk just before you hope it will affect you.

Many liqueurs are made aromatic with herbs. Izarra, whose name means 'star' in Basque, uses thirty-two Pyrénnéan herbs in its yellow version and forty-eight in its green one, sweetened with mimosa honey and distilled in a base of Armagnac. Try a *Green Beret Basque* – half green Izarra, half brandy. Stir in shaved ice and drink with a straw.

Aromatic vermouths are medicinal and stomach settling, and can be served as aperitifs with ice and soda water, or neat as digestifs. Appetite whetting as they may be, some, like Fernet-Branca, Underberg and Amer-Picon take a strong constitution to imbibe, but are marvellous for settling a stomach.

Also aromatic, though not medicinal, is *Rose Water*, an age-old flavouring for drinks and desserts. To make it you fill a pan with petals, cover it with water and keep the water at boiling point for an hour. Remove the petals and add fresh ones. Keep this up until you reach the strength you want. Use the rose water with vodka in a tall glass, or to flavour ice cream. Almonds and pistachio nuts, saffron and rose water, honey, mint and a whole Arabian Nights' entertainment of flavourings and aromas can be used in beverages not only to change your gastronomic life for the better, but to give a completely new dimension to liquid refreshments as well.

It is a comforting thought that it is one of the easiest things in the world to make drinkable alcohol. But there is one slight drawback. Making it without official permission is verboten. Until recently, however, you were allowed to make your own eau de vie in France if you had fruit trees. So, when I lived there (and saw to it that I did have fruit trees), I took advantage of the opportunity afforded me by the benevolent French and made my own 'white alcohol'. The process is simple. You get a barrel – mine held twelve gallons – and wait for the fruit to ripen and fall off the trees. Then you stuff the barrel full in the autumn and wait for the mess to ferment, which takes two or three weeks. The best results come from sticking to one kind of fruit – plums, for instance – but you can use whatever you have – pears, apples, cherries, peaches, plums, even berries.

My fermenting overflowed and made the cellar smell marvellously heady. When that stopped, I bunged the barrel and left it until spring to meld. Then came the wonderful Frenchness of the process. An itinerant distiller came to the village, and I took my perfumed barrel and a few clean wine bottles to him. He poured the fermented mash through a sieve into his boiler and, in a few hours, it went up into the cooling coil in the form of steam, then down in condensed drips into my bottles in the form of what can only be properly described as firewater!

This did not discourage the local gipsies, who would lie under the spout with open mouths to catch the last drops. They were strong, pure, colourless alcohol but, even at that stage, quite drinkable and with an aroma that was even better than their taste. Professional distillers have more experience with such things, and their concoctions may be smoother than my do-it-yourself liqueur was, but it was mine, all mine, and I loved it.

The principle is the same for making all fruit or grain alcohols. No matter what you start out with, the end product is always a clear, water-like liquid.

The French, as usual when it comes to affairs of the stomach, are very logical and practical. In Alsace, where some of the best of the fruit brandies are made, it is the Civil Engineering and Country Highway Department that controls the vintage of black cherries, pears, wild strawberries, raspberries, and other local fruit. This is because so many fruit-bearing trees line the roads and canals. During the war my friend Lee Miller, a fabulous photographer, gourmet, and war correspondent for *Vogue*, of all unlikely jobs, once came upon a cache of superb framboise during an advance. GIs were swarming all over the cellar of one Alsatian distiller, enjoying, but not really appreciating, the contents. Lee, with great aplomb, 'liberated' a Red Cross jerry can, meant to hold sterile water, painted it khaki, filled it with framboise, and the supply went with her, posing as gasoline, from then on. Petrol was supposedly

5

more precious than fine gold in those days, so no one was surprised that she should nurse the jerry can so carefully. It did astonish them to see her take a swig of it from time to time. Only the magic correspondents' circle knew that the French equivalent of Southern Comfort was in that treasure can. As the level of framboise dropped, Lee refilled the can with whatever else she could rescue, and ended up with the most horrendous cocktail ever. Fortunately for her, she never had hangovers.

The thing that possibly gave her confidence about treating fruit brandies like that, not to mention gin, vodka, and most of the drinks or liqueurs made by distilling, is that they all started out as medicine. Even vodka began life as a preventative for flu.

The Arabs were the first to discover the distilling process (the word alcohol itself stems from Arabic), and travellers brought this Eastern concoction to Europe where the medieval alchemists first used it in their search for the secret of eternal life. Distilling was the monopoly of the chemists and the liquors then made were called eau de vie, or 'water of life'. Because of its supposed healing qualities and because medicine was mainly in the hands of the religious orders, ownership of the stills tended to shift from the scientists to the theologians, so monks gradually got into the liquor business and roots, bark, leaves, rinds, nuts, herbs, fruits, juices, gold dust, coffee – you name it – everything was tried, not only for taste, but for medicinal effect. Thus there came to be hundreds of liqueurs and that is why so many of them have 'religious sounding' names – Benedictine and Chartreuse, for example.

Our forefathers all thought of liqueurs as potent medicines. They were an agreeable means of warding off fever and because of the soothing herbs in so many of them they came to be known in France as digestifs. 'Cordial', a similar term, is derived from the Latin word for heart and was originally used as a heart stimulant.

Aquavit, a caraway flavoured gin, follows the same tradition for its name also means water of life and caraway seeds are even now used in some countries as a pacifier for babies. Aquavit is practically the Scandinavian national drink, always taken with food, often served frozen in a block of ice, and goes wonderfully with smorgasbord. A *Danish Mary* is a good starter, made like its cousin Bloody Mary with tomato juice and Worcestershire sauce, but with aquavit instead of vodka.

Heaven preserve you or me from trying all the kinds of 'white alcohol' that exist. But some of them are worth tasting, and many of them add a wonderful flavour to food. In addition to kirsch, mirabelle and framboise, there is a delightful spirit made from Williams pears. Even if you have hay fever, the bouquet of the luscious pears get through. You may have tried pineapple with kirsch, but you have never really tasted pineapple unless you have had it with Williams. The two go together like Fortnum and Mason, but taste better.

The taste of kirsch, made from wild cherries, varies according to the amount of pits crushed with the cherries in the fermenting process. It takes sixty pounds (27 kg) of raspberries to make one bottle of the pot-distilled nectar known as framboise. The same for fraise des bois, made of wild strawberries. Mirabelle and quetsch, like slivovitz, are made from plums – golden plums for the first and small blue ones for the second. The juice is fermented, then double distilled with pits, to give a fine bitter tang to the liqueur.

Kummel is made with that excellent digestive aid, caraway seeds, and began life in Holland, but was made famous when Peter the Great of Russia, who worked incognito in the Amsterdam shipyards, chose it as his particular tipple. Russian Allash kummel is the best known, but is now made only in Germany. The Far East weighs in with sake, a sort of beer, from Japan, and Ng-Ka-Pe, Sam-Shu-Y and Mai Tai, rice spirits, from China.

Then there is slivovitz, the Balkan favourite, made of blue plums called sljiva. Some of the plum stones are crushed and their juices fermented to give the concoction an almond flavour. It was a slivovitz bottle with which a distinguished ambassador to Yugoslavia, shortly after the war, crowned a man during an encounter in a Zagreb bar – an engagement that became known as the 'Bottle Battle of the Balkans'.

Arack, Arabic for 'juice', is fermented and distilled coconut milk, dates or rice, depending on the area it comes from. The best is Indonesian. Tequila is made in Mexico from the heart of the century plant and, practically speaking, only drinkable preceded with lime and salt. Anis from Spain is made with aniseed. In short, there are hundreds of white spirits, including boukha, a North African fig drink.

Wine is ninety per cent water. White alcohol is just the reverse. Wherever you are in the world, you can enjoy very high spirits indeed by sticking to the countless varieties of 'eau de vie'.

The Bold Approach
to Sherry Drinking

Scotch Bonnet, Tipsy Cake, Gelée aux Xeres,
Cowshot, Sherry Puff, Sherry with Orange,
Sherry Flip, Green Knight, Bamboo,
Reform, Straight Law, Ship,
Mongole Soup, Leek Soup

People seem to think of sherry as a rather sweet, effete beverage. This of a drink made in the land of bullfighters, bull raisers and nerveless horsemen, where men are caballeros and the women adore the whole idea. Actually it is the most masculine of wines. Some of the best is as dry as a bone.

After years of finding my taste buds anaesthetized with cocktails, I finally discovered the super substitute for martinis – the perfect preprandial drink – a really arid sherry on ice. A Spanish fino is completely dry, has a light straw-colour look, a clean bouquet and a marvellous taste.

The Spaniards like their sherries chilled. I agree, especially for the dry ones. Taken, as I like it, on the rocks, you can even fool yourself into thinking that the fino you are enjoying is a martini, but instead of an 80 proof drink you are sipping 30 proof at a time – a distinct advantage if you have a prolonged cocktail hour.

I would hate you to be hidebound about types of drink, though, so I don't suggest sticking to one particular variety of sherry. There are sherries for every time of day – aperitif sherries, after-dinner sherries, sherries for drinking the whole meal through, winter sherries, summer sherries, sherries to flavour cooking with and to savour the cooking with. So the bold approach to sherry drinking is needed. Let your palate roam and compare and gain a new taste experience.

Real sherry comes only from Spain, and a very small part of Spain at that, around Jerez on the south coast. Not far from its vineyards is Cadiz where Columbus set sail for America. It is a blended wine, slowly and carefully done in kegs. The new wine is poured into the top cask of four or more layers of barrels that make up what the Spanish call a 'solera'. As the wine ages, it is siphoned from the top to the next layer and so on until it reaches the bottom. The younger wine is always mixed with older wines of the same type until it too is aged and ready to ship from the lowest row of the solera. About a third of the wine in the bottom row is taken off each year to send to your table.

One shipper I know said, 'I notice when I import a whole keg, that the blend always seems to improve toward the end of the barrel. They've enjoyed their marriage, I guess.' Actually the marriage is twice blessed, because sherry brandy is added to the young wines to produce the different sherry tastes. Export sherry (and this may be good news to some of us) usually gets more brandy than the stuff the locals drink. Vinegar made from sherry is the best there is, too, marvellously tangy.

A big outlet for certain sherries, which shall be nameless, is for altar wines in churches. Since more than half the total export of sherry goes to Merrie England, it is probably not surprising that the church trade in that land is brisk. One of London's specialists in sherry imports once found that a bill to a clerical customer was long overdue and finally sent off an invoice to the offending vicar with 'Urgent', 'Immediate Payment Requested' and other stickers all over it. What followed next makes for a rare vignette of British village life. It seems the vicar was horrified that the bill had not been paid but said that it was the fault of his predecessors. For years, apparently, the church treasurer, a Colonel J.P., Indian Army Retired (choleric), had won the village fair prize for fruit and vegetables, while his colleague and church secretary Miss S.T (acidulous), had won the prize for flowers. In the year of the overdue bill, 'by a total miscarriage of justice,' Colonel P. got *both* prizes. The result was that Miss T. and he ceased to be on speaking terms, and no church business got done! The vicar, however, added a postscript, 'You'll be glad to know the rift is now healed', and paid his sherry bill.

Only the ripest grapes are picked to make sherry. Once picked they are allowed to sit in the hot Andalusian sun to dry a bit. This concentrates the sugar in the grapes, before they are pressed into wine. After fermentation, some of the new wine develops a kind of bacteria on its surface called 'flor'. In other wines this would be a disaster, but in Jerez they want it to happen because – and this is one of the mysteries of sherry – flor is essential if the wine is to become a fino. So the vineyard owners encourage flor by not filling the casks to the top, and by leaving the bung open.

The shipper has to keep tasting the wine to see which type it may turn into. He must 'marry' the new to a similar older wine in his soleras. If the wine does not develop flor, all is not lost, for he can use it for some of the other types of sherry.

The Spanish are not heavy drinkers. They have a fear of drunkenness and they respect sherry. They usually drink it in a 'copita', a sort of extended onion-shaped, stemmed glass with a bowl about four inches high. They fill it only about a third of the way up so the aroma is concentrated in the narrow upper part of the glass. Thus as you are about to sip you get a sort of preview of the taste to come, and double enjoyment.

When finos become older and fuller in flavour, they are called 'amontillado', still a good light summer pre-meal drink, but a bit sweeter and perhaps more to the taste of the ladies. Winter sherries are the fuller bodied 'oloroso' and the golden 'amoroso', rich wines that make a splendid finish to a meal.

For the absolute tops in after-dinner sherries, in my opinion anyway, a tantalizingly dry-sweet and very old oloroso called Dos Cortados by Williams & Humbert would be hard to beat. Its label says it is a 'wine for kings' and I think the label is right.

The better sweet sherries, with dessert rather than aperitifs in mind, include Dry Sack and Harvey's Bristol Cream. A very good all-round sherry, if you can find it, is Don Zoilo – dry and very old and so clear 'it leaves no shadow'! For very dry drinkers, there are Tio Pepe and La Ina, a taste that is especially good as an aperitif.

Spanish sherry is the old original, but other countries produce wine like it. None, to my mind, tastes quite like the real thing; they don't have the native acidity of the Spanish ones. As the Spanish say, *El amigo y el vino antiguo* – friends and wine should be old – and that's the way I feel about sherry.

Sherry is often used in cooking. For this purpose, non-Spanish versions are okay. One cardinal rule in using sherry, according to a gourmet who lives not far from the sherry regions in Spain, is always to add the sherry at the last minute as it loses its flavour if it is heated.

At formal dinners in Britain, the consommé is often spiked with a jigger or so of sherry. This is probably the most primitive form of sherry cooking. If you are a Chinese food fan, sherry can be used instead of Chinese rice wine in any of their recipes.

My friend, Kenneth Lo, an expert on Chinese cooking, tells of a number of 'drunken' dishes that his compatriots make by marinating fish or meat or poultry overnight. Then after rinsing in fresh water the food is steamed or simmered quickly, drained, dried, and steeped in sherry. This steeping goes on for a week. The food is then cut into bite size pieces and eaten cold.

A good hot sauce for pepping up soups and egg or fish dishes is a *Scotch Bonnet*, made of sherry and peppers, and with something of the electric effect of Tabasco. Put enough small dry red chillies into a pint bottle to fill it a quarter full, then complete the filling with dry sherry (a cheap one will do).

Cover tightly and keep for two to three months, shaking occasionally. Pour out what you need into a sprinkler bottle, and sprinkle sparingly.

To go to the other extreme – the sweet end of the meal – sherry is a major ingredient of *Tipsy Cake*. For this you start off with a sponge cake, which you split in half. Spread each piece with strawberry jam, or apricot jam, or both. Put these in a serving dish and pour a quarter bottle of sherry over them. Leave for an hour. Make a binder by boiling a pint (6 dl) of milk and pouring it over four beaten egg yolks. Beat the mixture, and transfer it to a double boiler. Stir carefully over hot water until it starts to thicken. Take it off before it curdles, add a few drops of almond essence and two tablespoons of sugar. Beat again and pour hot over the cake. Let it cool then cover with whipped cream and put in the refrigerator until you need it.

The French make a *Gelée aux Xeres* thus: heat a pint (6 dl) of sweet sherry, the peel of a lemon and five tablespoons of sugar to simmering point and simmer for five minutes. Strain. Dissolve a packet of gelatine (one tablespoon) in a half cup of water in a bowl that is set in simmering water. Add the gelatine mixture and another cup of water to the wine mixture, pour into mould and cool. Serve with whipped cream.

You might try a *Cowshot* instead of breakfast one day if you are in a hurry. This is a Bullshot (see page 46) made with sherry, dry preferably, instead of vodka. As a hangover cure, a cup of hot beef consommé laced with something like Dry Sack might do the trick. And you can make a martini with dry sherry instead of vermouth – but not for breakfast. Or another quick, easy pick-me-up, the *Sherry Puff* – a glass of sherry with an egg beaten up in it – restores the circulation.

Like so much of what is best in the world of wine and spirits, Jerez owes much of its success to the indefatigable Anglo-Saxons. Some of the early sherry wine shippers were 'Wild Geese', the titled Irish who fled from Ireland in the late eighteenth century because Catholics were being persecuted. Many of the finest sherry houses have British sounding names like Gordon, Harvey or Williams. John Ruskin was the son of a sherry wine merchant, and he himself started out in the business.

Another foreigner is responsible, the story goes, for one of the main grape types in Jerez. He was Peter Siemens, a German sailor, who brought a grape to Spain that bears his rather Hispanicized name – Pedro Ximenez. This grape is used almost exclusively in Montilla, a wine very similar to sherry but grown near Cordoba just outside the legal limits for sherry in Spain. Amontillado sherry originally got its name because it tasted like Montilla.

Sherry wine, like champagne, is grown in chalky soil, but unlike its famous French cousin, it grows under a burning sun and scorching levant winds. And in spite of that, in September good sherry vines give the impression of having more bunches than leaves.

Sherry was once considered a splendid antiseptic and medically beneficial. A 'good sound sherry' was generally recommended for doctors and gin for nurses in Dickens' day. Perhaps that formula lies behind the British navy's macabre story about Lord Nelson, whose body was shipped back to England from Spain in a full cask of sherry to ensure its preservation. When the body was put into the keg, it was full. But when the barrel arrived in England all the sherry was gone. Had Nelson's ghost drunk the wine? What happened to it? '¿Quien sabe?' as the Spaniards would say.

Sherry has been a popular drink for centuries. The 'sack' that Shakespeare's Falstaff drank in such heroic quantities was almost certainly a strong sweet wine, something like our heavy brown sherries. Today, such a variety of sherry is produced that you should be able to find one to suit both your taste and your purse – and the occasion to boot. It goes well as an aperitif, with egg dishes and with cheese. Amontillados are excellent with strawberries. Fresh orange juice with a jigger of dry sherry in it makes a marvellous mid-afternoon refresher on a hot day. For a *Sherry Flip* you need one egg, shaken with ice, a teaspoon of caster sugar and a sherry glass full of sherry, strained into a glass and dusted with nutmeg. Or for a *Green Night* you need equal parts of dry sherry, vermouth and lime juice, topped with two ice cubes. You could decorate the mixture with a holly leaf and berry – but don't eat the berry! For a *Bamboo*, take half measures of dry sherry and of dry vermouth, add a dash of angostura and ice.

A *Reform* needs two parts sherry to one of dry vermouth and a dash of angostura. Stir with ice, strain and serve with a cherry for colour. Even less complicated is a *Straight Law*, which is two parts dry sherry to one of gin, stirred with ice and served, strained, with a twist of lemon. Whereas four parts of sherry to one of whisky, laced with a couple of dashes each of rum, prune syrup and angostura, for some reason makes a *Ship*. Shake with ice.

A good 'recovery soup' for four ailing imbibers is a *Mongole* – take a tin each of condensed tomato and pea soups, a small pot of single cream with an equal amount of water, a teaspoon of sugar, two teaspoons of Worcestershire sauce, salt, pepper, three tablespoons of sherry and a little soured cream. Combine soups and water in saucepan and heat slowly, stirring until smooth. Stir in cream, sugar, salt, pepper and Worcestershire sauce. Remove from the heat and add the sherry. Top each serving with a teaspoon of sour cream.

For *Leek Soup*, wash the white part of four big leeks and slice then cross-wise into thin rounds. Put them in a saucepan with two tablespoons of melted butter and a chopped onion. Sauté slowly until they are pale golden. Now add four peeled, diced potatoes, two and a half cups of hot water, salt and pepper. Simmer until the potatoes are tender. Add three cups of hot milk, a table-spoon of butter and stir. Add a teaspoon of sherry per portion and serve.

In any case, you might take a hint from the Andalusians for whom there can never be such a thing as a 'last drink'. Politeness decrees, they feel, that you cannot offer your guests a last glass of sherry. It is always *la penúltima* – next to last. At that rate, with luck you could be enjoying sherry forever.

Passionate Port

Revolution, Portcola, Port and Lemon Cooler,
Port and Orange Cooler, Port and Soda,
Port Cocktail, Devil, Port Flip,
Port Nightcap, Negus

Port is the most sensuous of wines. Even the adjectives used to describe it are voluptuous, smooth, seductive, velvety – sexy words that slide self-indulgently off the tongue, while the wine itself slides richly over it. It is an old-fashioned beverage to be sipped slowly, to be sat over for half an hour, or an hour, in perfect relaxation after a superb meal. It is one of the world's noblest wines.

Or is it? Some people think port, on the contrary, is a trendy modern drink to accompany wild schemes hatched over a conservative bottle of Director's Choice. Or that it should be treated disrespectfully like the French and Portuguese themselves do. Drink it cold, as an aperitif or on picnics.

Port starts as a rather purple, ordinary harsh table wine. Port shippers' skill blends this unpromising liquid, fortified by a touch of grape brandy, into a mellow Ruby, delicate Tawny, or venerated Vintage, with beautiful, subdued colours, wines that are often older than the people who drink them.

In 1703, the British, to spite the French with whom they happened to be at war, practically eliminated taxes on Portuguese wine. Trouble was the wine was barely drinkable and travelled badly. In desperation, some English business genius thought of preserving very ordinary Portuguese vinho by adding brandy to it. Much to his surprise and the delight of his countrymen, the process improved the wine amazingly, emphasised its natural fruitiness, and made it simpler to ship. In 1775, the vintage was already so exceptional that the shippers sent it to England unblended, to be bottled sediment and all, and become the first of the famous vintage ports that Englishmen have stashed away ever since in their cellars – often only to be drunk, after they faded away, by their sons.

The city of Oporto (simply 'the port'), from which the wine got its name, is where port shippers operate. They keep their wines in luscious-smelling lodges across the river from the city. Many of the lodges are owned by people with very Anglo-Saxon-sounding names, and this is scarcely odd considering the beverage was more or less a British invention.

Vintage port is made from the grapes of a single year, unblended, and the year must be exceptional. Vintage stays in casks only two or three years, so it has no time to throw a crust before bottling, thus it needs to be decanted. In the bottle, it goes on maturing and improving for fifteen to twenty years. Port, by the way, keeps for as many as six months once it is opened, so you needn't feel you have to gulp it all down immediately.

There are old ways of drinking port, and new. You can blast off into space-age mixes like a *Revolution* – two parts ruby port, one part vodka, in a tall glass, with ice and a splash of soda. A more establishment drink is a *Portcola* – three parts any cola drink, one part ruby port, garnished with cherries, pineapple chunks and ice. And a mixture of port and lemonade made with soda water is a great cooler at a tennis party. The same is true of ruby in a tall glass with ice, soda water, and a slice of orange.

The most sensuous of all ports is vintage, which should be treated with the respect due its years. Only four vintage years were declared by most growers in the port vineyards during the ten years 1960 to 1970 for example. From the turn of the century four of the greatest years for ports 1912 (gorgeous), 1927 and 1931 (magnificent), 1935 (sublime) – were poorish years for French and German wines. Since then, 1958, 1960 and 1963 have also been good for port but less so for the northern wines. Port growers must have quick heat at the right time, and not too much of it, while the northern vintners pray for a lingering, hot summer. If you are able to wait that long, by 1980 you should be able to drink a 'great' 1963, and a good 1970 a bit later!

A Portuguese wine worker can tell top vineyards from second-class ones by standing on a hill, in the light of the full moon, and noting which shine and which look dead. The dead-looking ones produce the best grapes. From these good vineyards, and from any others they may own, vintners and shippers are elected to membership in the Factory House, a club that is a sort of un-official museum of port in Oporto. The Factory House belongs to a dozen firms for which it was built towards the end of the eighteenth century and is filled with period furniture, hand-painted ceilings, and cases of antique china. All members upon election have to present the club with six cases of their vintage port. Just imagine the quality of drinking that goes on. Your hosts make you move from one dining room to another in order to be sure that food smells do not interfere with the port's bouquet!

Drinking port begins as a young blended wine, kept long enough 'in the wood' to lose its original purpleness. Bottled after two or three years, it is called ruby, the vin ordinaire of ports, less expensive than other ports because of its youth – less costly storage in its past. As it continues to age, bottled port becomes lighter in colour, 'tawny' in fact. A ten-year-old tawny Quinta do Noval is drier, smoother, and more elegant than a ruby, with a nutty flavour.

A twenty-year-old tawny is for connoisseurs – rare and lovely sipping. Late bottled port is comparatively young but kept longer in casks than ruby, five to six years, before bottling. Because this gives it time to throw its sediment, it does not need decanting, so is easier to save.

Crusted port is non-vintage. It can be a blend of wines of different years or of several vineyards but treated like vintage. There is also white port, made with white grapes and, as usual with white wines, separated immediately upon pressing from the skins, contact with which, white or black, gives wine its colour. White port is usually drier than ruby or tawny. Cold, it makes a wonderful aperitif, or with ice and soda water, a fine long drink.

One great British port connoisseur used to say that the time to drink the stuff is 'Now!' In his late seventies this man played golf and court tennis, worked three days a week, and did all this on a diet of tawny, which he claimed must always be drunk either at cellar temperature or chilled.

If you want your port mixed, the simplest *Port Cocktail* is two jiggers of port, a dash of cognac, stir with ice, strain into a glass, and squeeze an orange peel over the top. Nearly as easy is a *Devil*: one part port, one part dry vermouth, a dash or so lemon juice. Stir with ice, strain into a glass. A *Port Flip* uses two jiggers of ruby, one egg and a teaspoon of powdered sugar. Shake well with ice, strain into a glass and add nutmeg on top if you like it.

And before you retire in general, or to bed in particular, try drinking a good dollop of tawny port in a tumbler, filled with cold milk, and see how fast that gets you to sleep. For a warm nightcap to entertain several friends on a cold evening, try the *Negus*: two bottles of ruby, the grated peel of one lemon, the juice of two lemons, several cloves and a small stick of cinnamon. To all of which add a quart of boiling water.

NOTE Imitation is the reward of success, as the Porto Wine Institute, like many others, has discovered. It would now like its wine, made since 1746 only from grapes grown in a specified area of the Douro valley in Portugal, called 'porto' instead of the familiar 'port' to distinguish it from wines called port but made elsewhere usually from different grapes and by different methods. All genuine ports are labelled 'product of Portugal', and wines bottled and shipped from Portugal must be labelled 'vinho do porto', but ports shipped in bulk to England and bottled there need not be and are not. This inconsistency is what the Porto Wine Institute is attempting to sort out.

Champagne – Psychological Magic

Chilled Champagne Cocktail,
German Bowle, Random Punch, Lemon Punch,
Personal Punch Framboise,
Dragoon Punch, Black Velvet

At the tender age of sixteen, I was introduced to the astonishing psychological effects of the world's most joyful drink – champagne! One of my pals managed to smuggle back, from his sister's wedding to our staid boarding school, a beverage whose potency and erotic effects were claimed to be beyond even our wildest dreams.

Some eleven friends were invited to sample this elixir behind the school barn after lights-out. We gathered, shivering with clandestine pleasure and half drunk with anticipation. And a good thing too, for one bottle among twelve people – even of French champagne – does not generate much jazz. But the psychological effect was to sow the seeds of a series of memories that will certainly make me start up in my wheelchair at ninety-three.

There is nothing like true champagne to give you, personally, the feeling of being on top of the world, and to give the impression that you are not only a fine fellow, but rich and generous to boot!

True champagne – and I admit to being brainwashed – comes from one place only, although good sparkling white wines exist in other parts of the world. And that place is the region around Rheims and Epernay in France. If you are visiting France, you really should make the detour to visit the cellars. Some of them are works of art dating from Roman days. The Romans dug out the soft Champagne country chalk in a peculiar way. They began with a hole at the surface that looked as if it were a well. They then cut out the stone under this hole to make a sort of empty pyramid underground, with a base that sometimes measures fifty feet or more at the bottom, which itself is some thirty or forty feet below the surface.

The lower parts of these hollowed-out pyramids were connected at their bases to form a series of rooms. With their cone-shaped walls, and their beautiful rough white chalk surfaces, these strange quarries reach up towards the surface like nothing so much as cathedrals, cool and tranquil, and just right for the repose of the most regal wine there is.

In these stately cellars, and others built in the chalk in more modern fashion – 120 miles of them in all – over two hundred million bottles of champagne age and form bubbles, ready to tickle your nose and throat. Outside France the largest part of this store goes to Britain and America. Added to all the other kinds of sparkling wines you can buy – made in America, or Spain, or Germany, or Italy – the total of bubbling wine consumed in the world seems to indicate that in good times or bad a party is still a party is still a party.

Gertrude ('a rose is a rose is a rose') Stein's friend, the autobiographical Alice B. Toklas, was once my guest at a memorable picnic. We spent some time finding the perfect spot in her honour, and finally chose a handsome hillside near Montfort l'Amaury because we wanted everything, including the view, to be just right.

The big day showed up. We piled the magnum of cooled champagne, the food, mountainous Jim Beard, sparrow-like Alice, and ourselves into my tiny Fiat and took off for Montfort. Once there we spread out the rugs and a few pillows for Alice, who was well over seventy years old at the time, so she could get the best view of the lovely countryside. 'No,' said Alice, plumping herself down with her back to the whole valley spread before us, 'I never look at views. Spoils my concentration on food!'

That was my very first champagne picnic, and it de-snobbed the drink for me wonderfully. Champagne's renown as not only a delicious drink, but the drink of success can sometimes be a bit aweing. French or not, almost any champagne just can't help adding a kick to a picnic, a banquet or a dinner. Somehow – maybe it's merely the wine's sparkle – it will turn any kind of occasion into a party. If you have that bottle of bubbly on ice when unexpected guests drop in, it is one of the easiest, yet most exciting ways to say welcome – and mean it.

Visually, the most impressive thing in the making of French champagne is the long, long cellar corridors filled with ageing bottles, but the next most interesting, I think, is the process for removing sediment. Once the bottles are filled up with wine, they get a temporary cork and are stacked on top of each other for about four years to mature. When the time comes to ship them off for sale, the bottles are stuck into a rack with specially shaped slots that allow them to start off flat, and be gradually up-ended, until they are standing upside down.

An expert remueur, or juggler, comes along once a day, gives each ageing bottle a slight twist, and moves it so its cork is a tiny bit lower than it was before, thus sliding the sediment slowly down into the temporary cork. This takes about four months, then the necks of the bottles are frozen, imprisoning the sediment. Another expert, in one dexterous movement, uncorks the bottle. The gas shoots out the frozen plug of sediment. The bottle is then speedily recorked without a drop being spilled, and the champagne, limpid and luscious, is ready to drink. This method is fast losing place to mechanical remueurs, alas!

Champagne tastings are often put on by distributors in the bigger cities and you should try to take advantage of them. They give you a chance to sample the different wines. The best, I think, is what the French call 'brut'. It is the driest, and usually made without the added syrup used to sweeten some of the other types, including the one called 'extra dry'. By tasting the wines together, you can make up your own mind which type you would most like to buy and keep at home.

One huge tasting of French champagnes I went to in California was masterminded by Philip Brown, one of America's top food experts – but no meteorologist. The weather, he claimed, was sure to be marvellous, so we decided to hold the tasting outdoors. Naturally, when the day came, it turned out to be the coldest September 13 in California's history. The host, the guests, and the organizers spent most of the day looking for braziers to place around the patio to give the atmosphere something of the warmth the sun should have supplied. In spite of the weather, the tasters came in droves, in their overcoats and the occasion was a howling success because the circumstances were unique, the brazier flames adding to the conviviality and the wines tasting superb.

A champagne tasting at home, if you combine it with an oyster tasting, or a ham tasting, or a pizza tasting, can be great fun. The idea is to get as many different kinds of oysters, hams or pizzas as you can collect, not to mention as many types of champagne as you can afford. (I don't mean different brands I mean tastes – brut, extra-dry, dry, demi-sec, and so on.) As well as French champagne you should try German, American and Spanish sparkling wines to compare their tastes and prices.

In Europe an occasion is hardly considered official unless it is accompanied by a 'coupe de champagne', the wine for toasting any accomplishment, be it winning a literary award or a fencing match, or launching a ship.

Vintage years are not important in champagne because most is blended and carries no date on the label. Only when the shippers feel they have a truly great year do they declare a vintage. Champagne is made from both white and red grapes, though both produce white wine. The trick is to keep the skins from contact with the juice once the grapes are pressed. Since the war, there has grown up a fad for 'blanc de blancs', which means wine made from white grapes only. It usually costs more, but even an expert can't really tell the difference, so it is hard to see why it should.

As for the 'do's' and 'don'ts' of champagne – there are surprisingly few of the latter and it need not be given royal treatment when it comes to handling. Do, however, cool in an ice bucket, half filled with water and the rest with ice. And do take the cork out carefully, so as not to spill the wine. Popping the cork is great fun, and as long as you don't waste wine thereby the French attitude towards the pop is 'Why not?' *Don't* open warm or after being jiggled about, for then the champagne will spurt out half of its bubbles and waste a good deal of the wine. Although they object to swizzle sticks because 'it took four years to put the bubbles in', in summer the French have been caught putting ice in their champagne. Incidentally, they often judge it by its bubbles – the smaller the bubbles, the better the wine.

Why do people drink champagne when it is so expensive? I suspect it is partly because of its morale boosting quality. Partly also because it is like drinking liquid light. And partly because it tastes delicious. The French champagne producers had a survey made not long ago about French drinking habits and one question was what alcoholic drink they would choose for preference. Forty-three per cent said champagne.

Champagne, of course, is hardly the stuff to waste by pouring it into the slippers of the cast of *A Chorus Line,* but when you think that each bottle produces about eight wine glasses or slippers' full, the cost is not much more than a less prestigious drink. Champagne has always been expensive because it is costly to make, takes time to mature, needs skilled labour, and has a limited production since it only comes from one small area of France. On the other hand, it is a drink that can be used on every occasion, can be drunk throughout a meal and for social affairs has no serious rival. As the character played by David Niven in *The Pink Panther* said: 'Champagne isn't drinking, it's a minimum of alcohol and a maximum of companionship.'

Champagne comes in a crazy variety of bottles ready for any entertaining emergency with which you may be faced: there are splits, that are quarter bottles for solitary drinking, half bottles, Imperial pints (just right for two) magnums (2 bottles), Jeroboams (4 bottles), Rheoboams (6 bottles), Methusalems (8 bottles), Salmanazars (12 bottles), Balthazars (16 bottles) and, biggest and rarest of all for serving up to forty people, Nebuchadnezzars (20 bottles). The labelling is even crazier: brut is the driest although the word really means 'untampered with'. Extra-sec, although it should mean very dry is sweeter than brut, and sec even more so. Demi-sec is distinctly sweet, and doux exists but it is too syrupy for most tastes.

Mixing champagne with other wines, or with alcohols can be lethal, except perhaps in a *Champagne Cocktail*. One version is to place a small sugar lump in a tulip-shaped champagne glass, with a dash of angostura, and a twist of lemon and fill it (two-thirds full only, as with any wine drink) with chilled champagne. Some people 'improve' this by adding a measure of brandy.

Drinking champagne straight is a pleasure, but you may well like to try a mixed drink or two. One of the simplest, and one of my favourites, is what the Germans call a *Bowle*. You take about a pound (450 g) of fruit – best are sliced peaches or strawberries – and sugar them. Then pour half a bottle of still white wine over them and let them soak for a couple of hours. After that you add up to three bottles of iced champagne. The same thing can be done in smaller quantities as long as the proportion of fruit is about right.

Champagne Punch is another favourite of mine. Combine in a glass bowl half a pound (225 g) of caster sugar, two measures of cognac, two measures of maraschino, two of curaçao and three of lemon juice. Squirt in a siphon of soda. You can use the squirt to mix things up but if you don't, give the mixture a stir before adding a block of ice. At the last moment, before serving, add two or three bottles of champagne. This (let us call it *Random Punch*) is just one of a number of champagne punches which usually have a basis of orange or lemon juice, a measure of alcohol and from two to three bottles of champagne. They can be made in any quantities – from enough for fifty people or more (a gallon serves about thirty-two punch cups or about twelve people) down to a punch you can make for yourself if you're feeling lonesome.

For a good tart punch try combining three cups of lemon juice with half a cup of icing sugar, in a punch bowl with a block of ice. Add to this half a pint (3 dl) of maraschino and one pint (6 dl) each of curaçao and brandy. Now pour in three bottles of champagne and move it around gently so as not to eliminate the bubbles. Decorate each glass with fruit (if you like) and serve.

Slightly less sharp but quite delicious is this *Personal Punch*: fill a glass with ice, add a measure of framboise and the juice of half a lemon. Fill with cold champagne and garnish with a slice of lemon. Whereas for a party of twenty or so you might like to try a *Dragoon Punch*. To make this you pour three pints (1·7 l) of porter into a punch bowl, with three more of ale, and half a pint (3 dl) each of brandy, sherry and sugar syrup. Add thin slices of three lemons, a block of ice and last, two cold bottles of champagne.

Finally, for something quite different, but still using champagne, why not try a *Black Velvet* – half champagne, half stout – reminiscent of the good old Somerset Maugham days.

A word of warning: don't hoard champagne. It doesn't go on improving indefinitely like some great red wines do. It keeps for about ten years or so. I have had some very old champagnes that were still sparkly, but they had never left the makers' cellars. Old champagne can be great. It goes brown with age, and turns sweeter and heavier – a condition known as 'maderization'. A bottle of this is of uncertain quality but, if you are lucky, it can be a real taste thrill.

According to one English authority, a glass or two of dry champagne at eleven a.m. will do much to restore the damage caused by a heavy intake of alcohol during the previous night.

Well . . . it might be worth trying.

A Digression on Sparkling Wines

Practically every wine producing country has its sparkling wine. The French call theirs mousseux, the Germans sekt, in America it is American champagne (but the word American on the label must be bigger than the word champagne), in Italy it is spumante and in Spain champaña. Like champagne, these wines can be drunk throughout a meal, but are at their best as an aperitif.

The best of all, I think, comes from France and is made in the Loire valley – Touraine and Anjou. These vineyards, sprinkled amongst the lovely châteaux, are so far north that the weather is unreliable and the quality of the wine depends on the amount of sunshine in any one year. Without sun, or with too much rain, wines are very acid. This fruity but acid wine is perfect for turning into sparkling wine. The same is true of Alsatian and German wines which is why those parts of Europe also produce good bubbly. But then, so do Italy and Spain, where the sun shines unrelentingly!

I like getting a gift that I can immediately savour and share with the giver. In addition to setting a rollicking mood you are also doing yourself a favour when you buy a sparkling wine as a gift, for you will only spend half as much as for the same amount of a more expensive wine, and the effect will be even more convivial.

Two French sparklers that meet this double criterion and that I like as wines are Léon Gagnard, which comes from the Côte d'Or region and Blanc Foussy which comes in an impressive long-necked flask and is a lively wine – vin vif brut – from Touraine, the home of Rabelais. A good sparkling white Burgundy is Crystal Dry and Kriter Brut de Brut is another excellent, dry near-champagne. Speaking of dryness, by the way, sparkling Vouvray is inclined to be slightly less dry than other Loire and Touraine sparklers. Mousseux made from Muscat grapes is almost always on the sweet side. Also well worth trying are Veuve du Vernay, a well-known Loire name, and Doff Cuvée Extra from Alsace.

I have to admit to a certain prejudice in favour of dryness in a wine. Strictly speaking, German wines are not dry compared to a dry white French wine and I am therefore inclined to prefer French to German sparklers. However, that is a personal taste and has nothing to do with the quality of the wine.

Germany's sekt today is strictly controlled by law. If the label calls it sekt, your tipple will be quality sparkling wine that has matured for at least nine months in the producers' cellars. Higher quality sparkling German wine, made from sixty per cent German grapes is called praedikatssekt. Kupferberg Gold is a good sekt to remember and is made from Rhine grapes. Deinhard Kabinet is another. When the wine is made from one hundred per cent German grapes, the label announces that it is Praedikatssekt mit Geographischer Bezeichnung. This is supposed to be top quality in line with the dignity of its mouthful of a name. Schaumwein, the fourth official class of sparkling wine, is the least likely to be of gourmet quality because nothing is required of it, apart from bubbles.

Asti Spumante, the best-known name in Italian sparkling wines, is not made by the champagne method but in tanks. The Italian vintners claim, that for their product, the tank system preserves the fruit fragrance best. New Italian laws, similar to the German ones, now restrict the right of a wine to call itself asti. To have this on the label all the grapes used must have come from the district of Moscato d'Asti, in Piedmont, between Genoa and Turin. The best-known names in Asti are Gancia and Piccadonna.

In Spain the local champaña is dry and good for the price, but like most sparkling wines from outside France, it tends to be sweeter, and to taste better in Spain than it does when you get it home after a holiday. Perhaps the lightest and least alcoholic of the sparkling wines are the Portuguese white vinho verdes, made from slightly unripe grapes. These give a tartness and natural fizziness to the wine that makes it very refreshing on a hot summer's day. One of the best brands is Gatão, hard to find outside Portugal; but you will find Brillhante Seco, a natural sparkling wine, as well as Casal Garcia and Lancers.

Candy is Dandy
but Wine is Divine

(with apologies to Dorothy Parker)

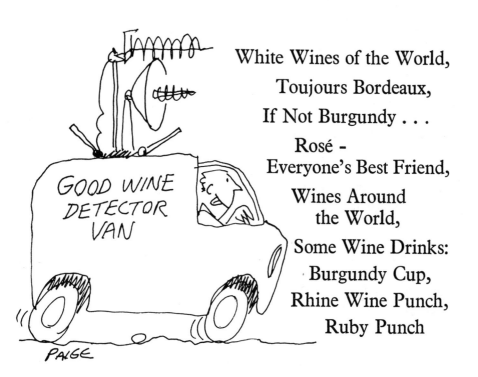

White Wines of the World,

Toujours Bordeaux,

If Not Burgundy . . .

Rosé –
Everyone's Best Friend,

Wines Around
the World,

Some Wine Drinks:

Burgundy Cup,

Rhine Wine Punch,

Ruby Punch

Learning to appreciate wine is a bit like falling in love. It happens to you without you actually encouraging it. But unlike love there is little chance that divorce will set in, unless your doctor intervenes. Drinking wine is addictive, once hooked, always hooked. At least that is what I have found.

White Wines of the World

I make no claim to wine expertise. I just like wine. My personal preference is for red over white, and French over others, and Bordeaux over Burgundy, to set things straight at the start. However, I have no intention of forcing these preferences on anyone. Wine is a wonderful drink, and as someone has said, no wine maker in his senses starts out with any idea except to make the best wine he can, and to make it as agreeable to drink as possible. And if you like Greek ouzo better than Château Courant d'Aire, you have every right to indulge your own fancy.

There is the contemporary and romantic view of white Burgundy wines as 'female, ladies of somewhat easy virtue, covered with jewels, sensuous, seductive', expounded by the French gourmet magazine, *Gault-Millau*. That's not bad either. Opinions range from this to the no nonsense approach of the American expert, James Beard, who says right out that the Côte de Beaune is 'notable for being the home of the greatest white wines in the world to my taste'. All this goes to show that the intake of wine information can be almost as sensual, sublime, and confusing as the intake of the wine itself!

Burgundy whites worthy of winning gold medals in the wine world Olympics include Pouilly-Fuissé, Meursault, Chablis, flinty and dry and just right for an oyster tasting, and, for my taste, the less aristocratic wines of the Loire: Muscadet, Pouilly Fumé, Sancerre. I especially like one that has not travelled much up to now, Saumur. Saumur is grown in an area that includes an atomic energy plant, some of the loveliest stretches of the Loire, and huge dank cellars from which the mushrooms you had recently with your steak probably come. The wine is light, muscat-redolent, and delicious.

By the way, grapes are the only fruit that will preserve themselves without any additives or subtractions. If you crush a bunch of grapes and leave the juice in a glass, it will turn to wine because grapes have fermenting sugar in them, and the dusty bloom on their skins has a natural yeast that can turn those sugars, through fermentation, into alcohol.

Wine, since the earliest times, has been considered an aid to good health. The French doctor who now claims it as the best of all medicines is only following in the footsteps of Galen, the Greek physician, who called it 'the nurse of old age' – an observation borne out by recent experiments in the States which have established the value of wine in the treatment of geriatrics.

Certainly there are wines that stimulate the appetite. Some are even said to be helpful in slimming – cutting down the body's need for starchy foods. Dry wines are said to be good for diabetics and all wines are relaxants as the French chemist knows to his cost: trade in tranquillizers is slow in a country where everyone drinks wine instead of water. (An Italian will tell you quite innocently that he does not 'drink' because he drinks wine and nothing else. A Frenchman might well do the same.)

But back to business – Bordeaux white wines used to be largely sweet, but today, because the market demands it, some of their new efforts are quite dry. Nevertheless, Sauternes remains a great sweet white wine, with Château d'Yquem at the top of the bin – excellent by itself, as an aperitif, or after a meal. Often Sauternes is drunk with a sweet dessert, but I prefer it by itself, or in a near icy state with caviar or foie gras.

After the French, my vote goes to the Italian whites. Verdicchio, from the 'calf' of Italy's leg, near Ancona, is a new wine, made only since the last war – not high in alcohol, light and dry and good with fish. Orvieto is another good wine, from just north of Rome, and should be drunk young. But my favourite is light, fragrant, Frascati from just south of the capital, where it is stored in the cool natural grottoes that Goethe once praised. Soave, from near beautiful Lake Garda, is perhaps the biggest selling of all Italian whites, and one of the country's best-known names.

Germany produces some of the finest white wines there are. I like to drink them on their own, rather than with a meal, fruit or dessert. Essentially I think they are to be enjoyed as a taste sensation, separated from the interruption of food. Take a Niersteiner Speigelberg Silvaner Trockenbeerenauslese, if you can pronounce it. It is almost a grape extract with a honey bouquet like raisins.

Fine German wines rejoice in one of the industry's most complicated bottling and labelling systems. Green bottles mean the wine is a Mosel, lighter, and less alcoholic than the brown-bottled Rhine wines, while a flagon-shaped bottle comes from near Würzburg, between Frankfurt and Nuremberg. There are three official qualities, ranging from the Tafelwein (table wine) through Qualitätswein (quality wine, with more body), to Qualitätswein mit Prädikat (Germany's highest accolade).

One advantage of German wines (as a matter of fact this is true of most white wines) is that they need no careful storage or special decanting. You can buy them on the way home, cool them and quaff.

Trailing along after the gold medal winners there are, of course, a host of very drinkable white wines. If you prefer light ones, try the Portuguese Vinho Verde. They have a slight tingling sparkle that is nice and fresh, and are low in alcohol.

White wines from the vineyards of the United States are also beginning to be better known. Their labels identify them by the name of the variety of grape from which they are made, such as Pinot Chardonnay, Sauvignon Blanc, Chenin Blanc, Riesling and Gewürztraminer. Most of them are pleasantly dry, but rather more potent than their European counterparts, averaging fourteen degrees of alcohol against ten to twelve for the average European product.

Spanish plonky whites ('Chablis types') abound, but Spain is better known for its reds. The only great white wine produced there is sherry – in a class by itself, and not really a table wine.

Dry and medium dry Hungarian Riesling exists, but the white wine for which Hungary is famous is Tokay, a luscious dessert wine, almost a liqueur. Production of this delight is long and costly, for the fermenting paste used to help make the wine rich and sweet takes up to seven years to work and, once it is added to the wine, four to eight more years in the cask before Tokay is put into its traditional half-litre bottles.

In the medium price league you can find reasonable Chilean, Australian, Hungarian, Jugoslav and Greek wines. Quality is inclined to vary considerably from bottle to bottle, and from grower to grower. The best thing in the case of such wines is to take the advice of your friendly local wine merchant, and be sure he is a wine drinker himself! Or take a good look at the name of the shipper. He tries to give his customers the best value he can. His name is your guarantee.

Toujours Bordeaux

It is not really necessary to be introduced to Bordeaux wine in France illegally, but it adds a certain 'je ne sais quoi'. I was lucky enough to have that pleasure because it was in 1940 in the unoccupied part of France that I first tasted Bordeaux. There was a delicious atmosphere of conspiracy about the occasion since although the wine was a perfectly legitimate, superb Château Latour, the food was all black market and there was a special savour in knowing we were breaking enemy-imposed rules as we feasted.

My first taste of red Bordeaux wine was notable also because my host was one of France's gourmet journalists. He had been at the restaurant well before meal time, tasting the dishes in the kitchen, and seeing to it that the wines were perfectly served, at just the right temperature. I fell in love with Bordeaux then, and am still enamoured.

This 'best wine in the world', as Henry James calls it, comes from the region around the city of Bordeaux on the West coast of France, a smallish area dedicated to the worship of Bacchus, and one of the most British parts of Europe (after all, it was British on and off for three hundred years until Joan of Arc managed to recover it for France). The countryside is covered with valuable vineyards, which bring wealth to their owners, and pleasure to wine lovers around the world. Bordeaux wines were known already to the Romans, and were written up by Latin poets as long ago as AD 310.

Any day along the Quai des Chartrons, which is the Fifth Avenue or Bond Street of the Bordeaux wine industry, you can hear names like Barton, Johnston or Lawton, and the inhabitants of many of the famous châteaux are descendants of immigrants from across the Channel, or from other equally under-privileged parts like Germany and the Netherlands, drawn there by the delectable aroma of wine, and the interesting colour of the money to be made from it.

The life of these wine merchants has hardly changed in the past seventy-five years. They have jealously hung on to their legendary social positions. The 'great old families' of the region have had a hard time adjusting to life in the twentieth century, they are still living – apart from a few more modern-minded ones – in the eighteenth-century style imposed on them by their surroundings. The so-called châteaux they live in, though not the fairy-tale castles one might expect, are nevertheless very handsome country houses indeed.

To be counted among the royalty of the Bordeaux wine trade, you need to have three basic qualifications. The claret nobility must be Protestant, in the wine trade and of foreign ancestry. Some of the 'French' shippers, despite having been born in France and speaking the language grammatically perhaps better even than the natives, still talk of Britain, or Scandinavia, or Holland as 'home', send their children to Eton and Cambridge, or the equivalent, and speak their grammatically perfect French with a strong foreign accent. The 'in' gang qualifies for top local social acceptance, while the 'out' gang, because it fails in one or other of the three essentials, does not.

To dine in one of the great Bordeaux homes is to go back a hundred years into history. The huge, wide table can easily seat twenty people. Guests are international, for claret is sold all over the world, and the agents and importers and wine buyers from Hong Kong, Argentina or New York visit Bordeaux regularly. The food, for Bordeaux is one of the gourmet capitals of France, can be superb and the wines incredible.

I was once lucky enough to attend a dinner in Bordeaux where the wines alone, had it been necessary or even possible to buy them in a restaurant, would have cost one hundred dollars, or fifty pounds, a person or more, and these were served by a small posse of white-tied, tail-coated waiters, discreetly gloved who in a mellifluous *sotto voce*, gave you the name of each wine and its vintage date.

This kind of gathering is not always staid, however. One time after a very congenial, informal dinner with one of the most respected shippers in the area, we were all sitting around the kitchen table for a chat and a final glass or two, when the host suddenly challenged us all to a jumping match. From a standing start, you were supposed to jump over the back of a kitchen chair, which was placed with its seat towards you. Try that when you've had a few glasses of Château Lascombes. I managed it. The famous shipper did too, though he cheated a bit.

The old-time methods are what made Bordeaux great, and I would be sad to see the old ways of working, or ageing the wines, of blending them, or bottling them as vintage specialities abandoned. Good wine names, like Barton, Hanappier, Lawton, Kressmann, De Luze, Schroeder, or Beyerman of the old guard, and those like Cordier, Borie, Dourthe, Delors or Ginestet of the new, are still very important to the proper continuation of tradition.

There is a good deal of hocus pocus about how and when to drink Bordeaux. From the point of view of the average user, deciding which Bordeaux to buy can be simplified somewhat if you will remember five names – the classified areas of Médoc, Graves, St-Emilion, Pomerol and Sauternes.

The Médocs, St-Emilions and Pomerols are mainly red, Graves are both red and white, while the best of the Sauternes are sweet white. The labelling of Bordeaux wines is done in accordance with the French *Appellation Contrôlée* system, which divides the wines into three categories – the regional name (Bordeaux), the sub-regional name (Médoc), and the name of the commune (St-Laurent).

The least pretentious wines of the region would be labelled simply, 'Bordeaux'. Higher on the quality ladder come those with the area names like Médoc or Graves. Then a step above them, come the commune names such as St-Julien, Pauillac, St-Estèphe or Margaux, and finally the château names.

Of the Médocs, which I think the best of Bordeaux, only four châteaux wines are classified as first growths. Lafitte, Margaux, Latour and Haut Brion. The characteristics of Médoc are a slight harshness compared to Burgundy, a lingering fragrance, a fine bouquet – which, as in any wine, is given off by volatile essential oils in it – and aromatic taste and mellowness.

Among the Graves (except for Haut Brion, which is confusingly classed as Médoc) there are no first growths, but there are some very fine wines, among them Château Carbonnieux and Château Pape-Clément, for example. Graves get their name from the gravelly soil in which the grapes are grown. The reds are soft, and the whites are of two kinds, dry and vigorous, and sweet and fragrant.

In the St-Emilion group, also unclassified, the Châteaux Cheval-Blanc, Ausstone, and Beauséjour are some of the fine growths. Pomerols, which are much like St-Emilion, but quicker to mature, include Château Petrus.

Red Bordeaux wines go well with any main course, except fish, especially when you want a lighter general effect. Contrary to what most people think it should be served comparatively chilly – cellar temperature, the French say – or about forty-six degrees Fahrenheit.

7

If Not Burgundy . . .

Red Burgundy was not always at the top of the wine lists. Back in the days of Louis XIV, the palace tipple was a still red wine grown in the Champagne country at Ay. It was Madame de Maintenon (never underestimate the power of a woman) who indirectly changed all that, for she made the King switch medical advisers. The new doctor advised the Sun King to drink red Burgundy instead of champagne – not because of its delicacy or flavour but because of its therapeutic value. Since then the soft, savoury smoothness of Burgundy, rather than its medicinal qualities, has brought it almost universal acclaim.

Because Burgundy is so far north, wine-growing there is difficult. The sun shines only intermittently and the required alcoholic content is hard to come by. The vines need more care to protect them from mildew, early or late cold snaps can wreck the crop of grapes. Thus it is not surprising that the best wines from the region, both red and white, are costly.

Since the end of the last war, the French are drinking their Burgundies young, partly because wine growers have not been able to keep enough vintages ageing. After the Axis and Allied armies got through with them there was little of the old vintages left. Also, before the war, the fermenting process was kept going for several weeks, much longer than it is today. The result is that today's vintages are lighter and quicker maturing.

The greatest Burgundies come from the Côte d'Or – the Golden Slopes – divided into two sections. These are the Côte de Nuits (famous for reds like Nuits-St-Georges, Clos de Vougeot and Vosne-Romanée), and the Côte de Beaune (famous for whites like Corton-Charlemagne, Meursault, Montrachet). Farther north lies Chablis, one of the most imitated white wines in the world, and the northernmost of Burgundies.

Beaujolais, although quite legitimately a Burgundy, comes not from the Côte d'Or area but from further south and is made from Gamay grapes, whereas red Burgundy is made from Pinot grapes. Most Beaujolais, in fact, is a blend of red wines from anywhere in the Beaujolais district, but some comes from *Appellation-Contrôlée* towns. Some of these special Beaujolais are Morgon, Brouilly, Fleurie, Moulin-à-Vent and Juliénas. These are usually slightly more expensive than ordinary Beaujolais, and well worth it.

Nowadays Beaujolais is often served very young, and chilled. As a matter of fact, one of France's great cooks, Raymond Oliver, says that all red wine should be served not at room temperature but at cellar temperature – that is, cool. So tastes are definitely changing.

Between the Côte d'Or and Beaujolais lie two other Burgundy areas, the Maconnais and the Chalonnais. Maconnais produces an excellent, dry white wine, Pouilly-Fuissé, flavourful and crisp, as well as Macon itself, of course, which comes in both red and white versions. The Chalonnais contributes two good wines, Givry and Mercurey, but their labels are rarely found outside France. Incidentally, although there are châteaux in Burgundy, none of them produce top grade wine, so don't think you are getting something special when you buy a Burgundy wine with a château label.

Burgundy, where two and three star restaurants are thicker on the ground than in any other region of France, has some of the best wine and food in the western world. The wines are both delicate and powerful, and the food is equally varied. Brillat-Savarin, one of the great chefs of all time, was a Burgundian and the first food fair in the world was held in Dijon, the 'capital' of Burgundy. Dishes cooked 'à la bourguignonne' are to be found on all good restaurant menus. This means a sauce of shallots and mushrooms, sautéed in butter and simmered in red Burgundian wine.

In comparison with Bordeaux, Burgundies are full bodied, slightly more alcoholic, very slightly sweeter perhaps, but friendlier and easier to get acquainted with, so to speak. Vintage Burgundy wines have never been officially classified, and are seldom owned by a single proprietor. Burgundy wine growers often pool their output and sell wine co-operatively, so the names of the shippers are important.

After the Bordeaux and the Burgundies, the wines of the Rhône further south with their dark, purply-red colour, have a headiness, and a fullness of flavour that makes them excellent with highly seasoned food. Of these, the Côte Roti (roasted slope!) produces two very good types – Hermitage and Châteauneuf du Pape. Again, since these wines are blends, the shipper's name is important. Don't let them get too old before drinking!

Rosé - Everyone's Best Friend

Rosé is a wine you can serve at any time, with almost any kind of food (except pickles and salads) without a single qualm about having made some terrible *faux pas* in doing so. It goes with all sorts of meals – possibly not as well as a red or white wine might – but in an agreeable and uncomplicated way, for all you have to remember is to chill it and pour it.

As rosé is comparatively inexpensive, it is an ideal wine for informal dinner parties, quick lunches, kitchen meals, picnics or just to drink on a hot day. It is a wine in which the grape skins have been allowed to rest just long enough, after crushing, to give the liquid a rosy tint. Usually light and often less alcoholic than its red and white cousins, rosé has a limited range of bouquet and taste, which is probably why the experts tend to look down their noses when it is mentioned, yet it can be a delectable drink. It comes from many sources these days and it is the French who tend to produce the best. One of the most famous is Tavel, usually of a higher alcoholic content than other rosés. It comes from the Rhône Valley and, like all pink wines, is drunk young and will not improve with age.

The French variety that I like even better is Rosé d'Anjou, soft, light, slightly sweet, from north of the valley of the Loire river. There is also a Rosé d'Arbois from the Jura mountains in the west of France near Switzerland. The best Italian pink wines come from around Lake Garda and are very pleasant to drink. Yugoslavia has a fruity, deep pink wine called Ruzica, and Chilean pinks are also available.

Portugal's slightly sparkling Mateus Rosé is very popular and it is also refreshingly light.

Wines Around the World

From Spain comes Rioja red wine, comparable to regional Bordeaux wine, smooth, with a sunny disposition. Like Bordeaux, it also improves with age, and is fresh and excellent as a table wine. The labels Marqués de Riscal, Marqués de Murrieta, and Pomal are among the best. Less well known abroad, but good as a light, thin, young wine is Valdepeñas from south-east of

Madrid. Similarly, Dão from Portugal – reminiscent of Bordeaux – is dark, tart when young, better value even than Portuguese whites.

Swiss wines are also pleasant to drink in everyday circumstances as are some Australian wines, though there is a labelling problem here. Many Australian wines are named after the grapes used to make them but other 'varietal' wines have inappropriate French names like Burgundy and Claret, which they don't really resemble. The best Australian reds use Cabernet and Shiraz grapes.

One of my wine-wise British friends says (and he is not inclined to be over-complimentary to things American) that he believes Californian wines will, in fifteen or twenty years, be as good as any European wine, and possibly even better. He thinks the US wines will be the criteria by which other wines are judged, somewhat as the French ones are today. Time will tell whether he is right, but meanwhile, American wines are coming into their own as worthy of gourmet attention.

American wines started out by trying to imitate European ones with California-grown 'Bordeaux' and 'Burgundy'. Nowadays, since they really can stand on their own, they are being given more believable labels, indicating the kind of grape used in their making. Zinfandel is one of these and is a uniquely American grape – 'California's contribution to the wine world'. It produces a light red wine that ages well. As for white wines, America produces a great variety – they are good wines, with a distinctive taste, and getting better yearly.

Austria, Yugoslavia, South Africa, Chile, Russia, China, Iran – the list of countries where wine is produced is much longer than you'd expect and there are pleasant surprises to be had from almost all of them. Some South African white wines, for instance, really are comparable to a good Alsace or Moselle wine, but you have to be in South Africa to enjoy them for they are made in small quantities and hardly exported at all.

Some Wine Drinks

When wine is used for mixed drinks, mainly punches and cups, your average bright barman will stick to the inexpensive bottles of either red or white, for the ingredients tend to mask the taste of any high quality wines, and they are therefore wasted in a punch. In the following recipes wine from almost any part of the world will do just as well as the wine actually named, as long as it has a similar style and bouquet. For Sangria, for example, it would be sensible to use a Spanish red. But for a Kir, use a good white.

Kir is probably the most popular of wine aperitifs. You will find the regular recipe on page 18 but an agreeable new twist is to use red framboise liqueur in place of cassis.

Burgundy Cup mixes a bottle of red wine – Burgundy preferred – a bottle of soda water, four ounces (125 ml) of sherry, one ounce (25 ml) each of curaçao and brandy, a sprig of fresh mint, a slice of cucumber. Let stand one hour, add sugar if necessary, a big chunk of ice, and serve.

Rhine Wine Punch needs three bottles of German or Alsatian white wine (or a similar fruity wine), one bottle of soda water, four ounces (125 ml) of brandy and the same of maraschino, eight ounces (225 ml) of strong tea. Combine in a punch bowl, sugar to taste, decorate with fruit as you wish. Set the bowl in ice, or drop in a block of ice, and serve.

Ruby Punch for eighteen needs two bottles of sparkling Burgundy, four ounces (125 ml) each of brandy, curaçao and raspberry syrup, the juice of two lemons and two oranges, a bottle of soda water. Mix all but the water and wine, which you add, with ice, just before serving.

PAGE

Wine Tasting
and Storing

and What to Drink with What

'Not fat enough, but certainly charming,' my neighbour remarked off-handedly. I looked around to see which of our lady wine tasters he was commenting on, when he spewed a mouthful of lovely Niersteiner Spätlese into a champagne bucket next to me. I realized then, that it was not a lady but the wine he was talking about.

The main drawback to wine tasting is that you are not supposed to swallow the stuff. Instead you swish it around, 'clockwise for German wines,' said my neighbour, 'counter-clockwise for French'. And you have to spit it out because, after all, there are twelve wines to taste and you do not wish to reel away from the cellar in an unseemly condition.

These particular twelve were neatly set out in well-hidden cellars tucked under London's Adelphi. Each wine was numbered, so there was no chance to taste (I almost said drink) the wrong one by mistake, though you might get carried away by the poetry of the wine descriptions.

It was a lesson in tasting vocabulary that improved my concentration wonderfully. One wine had a 'burnt taste', the next was 'charming and fruitier'; after that was the fatter one which was also 'ripe'. The accolade went to a 1971 Hattenheimer Pfaffenberg Riesling Auslese which was 'perfect', with a lovely clean fruity acidity. I couldn't have said it better myself!

Sip, swill, aerate, pause and spit are the five rather unattractive sounding activities that, together with sniffing and looking, make a wine taster, but they do not confer instant expertise. Tasting is a professional business. A real taster sips, etcetera, between twenty and eighty different wines a morning, and a great deal of what he tastes ends up on our tables as plonk, for even plonk needs to meet certain standards.

A wine taster is no magician but by dint of much wine bibbing, he or she certainly can get to know a great deal about wines; what makes them good, which are likely to improve with age, and which are the best buys. Even the experts, many of them, can be fooled, and the ultimate decision for each taster or each appreciator is his or her own personal preference.

So as not to be intimidated by the knowledgeable, it is useful to have some system for tasting wines – either for fun, or to help you decide which to buy – so that you know what you consider good, and why. Of course it is preferable to begin by having a selection of wines to taste (and perhaps your wine merchant will oblige with some he would like to sell you).

The next essential is to have a glass in hand, half filled with the wine you are judging. Tasting is a sort of catch-all word, for the art involves sight, smell, and touch, as well as taste. Hold the glass to the light and try to decide if, in your eyes, its colour is right in relation to its type. A light wine should be clear. A full, warm one should look bright, and a rich deep wine's colour should almost sparkle.

Next, swirl the wine in the glass and sniff it. Decide what you think of its aromatic qualities: no bouquet at all, a fresh one with a touch of character, delicate, strong, fruity, spicy or exquisite and exciting? Then its taste. Take a sip but don't swallow it. Swirl it around and spit it out. Is it agreeable, fresh, light, robust and rough, robust and mellow, or fine or great?

Take another sip and ask yourself about its sweetness, acidity, texture or body, what it feels like in your mouth. (Some wine is so full bodied you can almost chew it.) Does it seem strong enough in alcohol? And what about its age? Does it seem too young, or is it mature, or at its peak? Textures, the touch part of tasting, can range from thin, through smooth, to full and, finally, superb.

If you are really being serious, number each of the items in the different categories and jot down those you decide fit the wine you are tasting. By then adding up the total, you can score your own opinion of each wine. Later you can compare its score with those of others you try. Better still, have a tasting party, and let your guests give their ideas about the wines you present them with.

This can be both fun and practical in helping you choose what you want to buy and what to drink with what. It may help to think in categories – the everyday, inexpensive wines to drink with family meals; next, the middle range of good wine to use at simple parties without being too ostentatious; and finally, a few great wines for the special guest, the connoisseur, and to go with food that is particularly good.

All wines are better off, cheap or dear, if stored on their sides. Resting on its side gives the wine components a better chance to meld into a harmonious whole. When the wine, especially red wine, is of good quality it often has a deposit which is the life blood of the more slowly maturing wines. A couple of days before drinking such a wine, bring it into the dining room and stand it upright to let the deposit (or dregs) settle to the bottom of the bottle. It is good to uncork all but the very oldest wines (whose bouquets may be too feeble to stand the air) half an hour before drinking. Ordinary red wines often benefit from two or three hours' exposure to soften and expand their flavour.

Decanting is another way to soften young wines, and is also sensible with old ones that have a deposit. You pour from bottle to decanter with a light behind the neck of the bottle to help you see the sediment. When the dregs reach the neck stop pouring. You can pour some of the wine that is left into another container and use it for cooking but throw away the final dregs.

There is no harm in leaving white wine in the refrigerator for an hour. Longer risks its absorbing odours (for don't forget that the cork is porous). Even in the freezer a bottle comes to no harm for a quarter of an hour or so, but take care it doesn't freeze for then the wine will probably be ruined – and champagne may explode!

Don't use metal goblets for wine, not even gold or silver ones. They may look nice but are disagreeable to drink from and prevent you from seeing and enjoying the colour of the wine. This applies equally to coloured glasses.

Moderate drinking, according to Dr Francis Anstie, a Scot who set his 'safe' limits a bit more than a hundred years ago, means taking in one and a half fluid ounces of alcohol a day – about half a bottle of wine, or two pints of beer, or three small whiskies. Dr Anstie also said that drink should be taken with meals, and the whisky thoroughly diluted. A more modern limit is that of Dr Maury who says that one litre per person per day is about right. American studies of drinking habits bear these medicos out. Recent research confirms that moderate drinkers tend to live longer than either heavy drinkers or total abstainers.

So try a tasting, drink moderately and be happy. As one of Britain's top wine experts, has said, wine is 'a most civilized drink, and the most productive of camaraderie and good humour'. I agree both with this and that other ancient dictum: 'In vino sanitas.'

All wine should end up being drunk so you should consider the shape of your drinking life before you really begin to build up a cellar.

For one thing you may easily stash away more wine than you can drink. For another, vintages change with age, so you need to sample your laid-down wines from time to time to check how they are getting along. Cellar conditions – often nowadays no more than cupboard space in a crowded flat – may not be perfect and will play a part in what happens to stored wine. Reds behave differently to whites. Price is not necessarily a guide to what is good. In short, there are no rules that always apply.

The ideal 'cellar' is very rare. Theoretically it should be underground, have a north–south circulation of air, be set away from tremors and noise and maintain a steady 10–13 centigrade temperature all year round. It should also be dark, have an earth floor and a high (70 per cent) degree of humidity.

Try to find that in your multi-storey flat. It is obviously not possible. But there is hope, for long experience has shown that by storing a small number of wines – say under a hundred bottles – and not storing them for too long, you can get away with far from ideal conditions. The main thing is to keep your wine away from excessive heat, which ages it too fast. If you can spare the space, an insulated cupboard with an air hole or two, and a holder for either a dish of water or a wet sponge to keep up the humidity, is a good substitute for a real cellar. You must keep the bottles on their sides, of course, so their corks stay wet and seal the contents from the air; and try to avoid places where there is constant jiggling from traffic or lifts or trains or whatever. Also avoid places with strong smells and remember to remove the paper wrappings off any bottles you store for they attract mildew.

Now for the contents of your mini cellar. Make a simple calculation. Suppose you drink half a bottle a day per person, minus holidays away and meals out, plus extras for parties. That would mean, for two people, something like two hundred bottles a year. Most of that would be vin ordinaire, for you probably drink plonk at home.

For parties, however, you would want to have some fine wines. For one thing the better the wine, generally speaking, the longer it will keep. The most economical system then, if you have the cellar space, is to buy the wine soon after it has been made and let it age. Such wine also improves in value. A good vintage is almost always a good buy, but before buying you should taste it and compare it with similar wines of the same vintage, for all of them are not equally good.

An exceptional vintage may not mean a better taste than a good or very good vintage, but it does mean that the wine should be at its best for a longer period of time. For most white wines, even the best, age is not so important. They get smoother, but may lose some freshness, except for those like sweet Graves and Sauternes, and Vouvray, which do not improve with age. Good 'bourgeois' red wines will ripen earlier than the 'greats' and last less long. Fruity wines should be kept only two or three years before drinking – Reislings and Gewürtztraminer (which are white) are exceptions and some of them will last twenty years, producing an increasingly exciting bouquet.

Great Bordeaux wines take about ten years to peak after vintage. Some last much longer. A great Burgundy lasts slightly less, say seven or eight years, before it begins to go off, but like Bordeaux will be drinkable for ten to fifteen years thereafter.

Dry white wine does not improve as much as reds with age. So you needn't keep much of it in your cellar. Buy it as you need it. Vintages are a tricky business and quality can vary from producer to producer. So, if you don't known yourself, you should find a good wine merchant to help you.

What to Drink with What

As for what wine goes with what food, you won't need any help with this, because with the possible exception of Grand Médoc premier cru and roll-mops, most wines go well with most foods. Almost all the rules laid down in the past hundred years about the absolute necessity of drinking white wine with fish, or red with game, can be disproven simply by experiment. But, after that very sweeping statement, I must caution you that there are some classic taste harmonies it is worth at least knowing about. These harmonies between certain wines and certain foods have, over the centuries, undergone experimentation by trial and error and do indicate what most people prefer. Still, taste is a very personal affair, so if you happen to like Bordeaux with your trifle although you may be in the minority, no one can say you are wrong.

In most cases the traditional matchings of wine and food are worth consideration, but it is also worth adopting the new trend toward experimentation in cooking to wines. Try cold Beaujolais with oysters, for instance, or a sweetish Sauternes with roast duck. Why not? You probably like duck 'à l'orange' anyway. At least you can claim to be inventive, even if you decide you do not like it.

To help you make the grand leap forward from routine into gastronomic adventure, there are some suggestions as to what to try with what that are not absolutely outrageous, but may nevertheless procure for you a reputation for audacity.

With seafood and oysters, for a start, the usual and excellent choice is a dry white wine, light, acid and not too fruity, like a Muscadet. A Reisling, either German or Alsatian, goes well too and – possibly slightly less so because it can have too strong a bouquet – a Chablis. You can also drink cold red wine with shellfish, a young claret, or a Beaujolais Nouveau. Nearly as daring, for the very reason that it is a fruity wine, would be to use one of the great white Burgundies, Corton-Charlemagne, a wine so perfumed that some people claim it tastes almost like cinnamon.

With smoked salmon and smoked fish in general, or with caviar (if you are an oil millionaire), no wines go really well, certainly not red. Best with these is vodka, or aquavit or schnapps. If you insist on wine, a Blanc de Blanc from the Champagne region is probably the best, or champagne itself.

Another problem is cold lobster, crayfish or crab mayonnaise, which taste best with a Sancerre, Pouilly-Fumé, an Alsatian wine, a German white or an Italian Soave – one of the fruity wines, in short. Boiled or grilled, shellfish seem to need one of the great white Burgundies like a Pouilly-Fuissé, a Musigny, a Meursault, or a Château Carbonnieux from the Bordeaux Graves region. The latter, by the way, got its name because, to avoid the Moslem restrictions on wine, it used to be shipped to Turkey labelled 'carbonated water'. If shellfish is cooked in a piquant sauce Armoricaine, a Sauternes or Monbazillac is the wine to drink.

With fish, I think it best to stick to the white wines. Sometimes it is fun to try one of the less dry types, like Sauternes, or a great Burgundy with a powerful bouquet like Montrachet (but since Montrachet itself produces only about a thousand cases of wine a year, your chances of doing this often tend to be limited by the cost). Actually, I like a light white Italian Frascati such as Fontana Candida, with most fish dishes. Champagne, I think, is wasted on fish, as it is on game and cheese.

Strangely enough, foie gras – though so marvellous in itself – is hard to match with the great red wines. So the 'plonkier' reds are to be recommended, or a powerfully perfumed white like a Traminer from Alsace, Germany or

Austria. Best of all, perhaps, is to drink port (a Quinta do Noval, say) with foie gras.

Jugged hare and other game animals need a good strong red wine like those from the Côtes de Nuits, a Clos Vougeot, or a Gevrey-Chambertin. The good Italian Chianti Classicos like Castello di Uzzano marry nicely with game, too.

For game birds, it is wise to match the strength of the wine to the colour of the meat when cooked; the darker the meat the stronger the wine, and the lighter the meat, the lighter the wine. A grouse or pheasant for example would take a Côtes de Nuits Burgundy or a Chianti Classico, a pigeon or quail might taste better with a Pomerol, or a Spanish Rioja, or an Italian Valpolicella.

For roast fowl and roast lamb the clarets come into their own. Médoc and Graves especially, but St-Emilion and Pomerol are good, too. As to grilled or roast red meat, steak or roast beef, here I would stick to tradition and red wine, putting the château-bottled red Bordeaux wines first partly because they can usually be relied upon to be what they say they are, but mainly because they are so good. After them come the great red Burgundies, of which the same could be said – they too are superb wines, destined by the gods to go with red meat.

Cheese is supposed to bring out the taste of wine, but to my mind this isn't always so. One of the 'smellier' great cheeses like a ripe Camembert or Pont l'Evêque or Munster has a strong taste of its own that kills a fine wine. So I would recommend the coarser, tougher wines like those from Spain, or some of the Italian ones, or a Châteauneuf-du-Pape with this type of cheese. Goat cheese goes best with dry wines that have a distinct bouquet, like Sancerre. And with Roquefort, my favourite cheese, as with blue cheeses in general, I like a sweet wine, a Sauternes or even port.

Salad is a food that, along with chocolate and hard boiled eggs, it is almost impossible to marry with wine because in its case the vinegar in the dressing kills the wine's taste. About the only wine that is drinkable with salad is the newly popular Beaujolais Nouveau. But truly, with salad, water is best. Save the wine for the cheese.

Champagne is one of the few wines that weds happily with sweets and puddings. Sherry will pass at times, or a liqueur. But I am not in favour of sweet wines with desserts. These are best sipped and enjoyed separately after the meal is over.

A Liquid Form of Summer

Singapore Gin Sling, Sundowner, Euphoria,
Tea à la Russe, Mexican Peter, Perroquet, Golnar,
Pink Fizz, Dubonnet Orange Fizz,
Dubonnet Whisky Fizz, Sangria, La Rose Americaine,
Coolers, Cannonball, Yellow Parrot,
Advocaat Lemonade, Orange Fizz, In Drink,
Zombie, Hop Toad

The sun is just going down like thunder in Sumatra 'cross the Straits. You are sitting on the veranda of Raffles Hotel, with Somerset and Sadie, swapping yarns and talking over the old days when you were a white hunter in your spare time and a rubber plantation boss when you weren't on the prowl. 'Mr Mitty,' he says to you, 'or may I call you Walter? Do you know how they make these teddibily tasty tipples we are sipping?'

You swirl your *Singapore Gin Sling* slowly around in your glass (it is too demmed hot to do anything fast), and drawl, 'Well, Somerset, old boy, the uninstructed tout various recipes, but my favourite is two measures of Tanqueray gin, the juice of one lemon, a measure of cherry brandy and a teaspoon of sugar.' You pause for effect at this stage, and eye the sinking sun. 'Then I consider a dash of Drambuie, and another of angostura essential – all well shaken with ice and poured without straining into a tall glass. A squirt of seltzer, and finally – note this – a thin layer of port wine to float on top.'

You lean back and watch the expression of adoration on Sadie's face, and awe on Somerset's, almost immediately falling off your camp chair, in time with the sun's disappearance, because this is the ninth sling you have slung.

For me, summer drinking is like that – a crazy, wonderful, never-never land of nostalgia and make-believe. Summer drinks either remind me of places I've been to, or of places I wish I had been to. And they are one of the reasons I enjoy moving out of the gloom of winter and into the bright hope of heat.

Summer makes me wish I were in a sea dragon shaped boat, with silk curtains to draw, shutting out the altogether too fantastic view of the Yangtse Gorges, sipping jasmine tea and rice wine. Where I am, however, is where I am and the thing is to make the best of the non-peripatetic life by a global tour of summer drinks into fabled lands of the vinous world.

First we should get ourselves into the right relaxed mood. It is an old French custom to keep a bottle of orange flower water on hand for calming hyperactive nerves. A very special one is concocted in Paris by Tanrade, near the Place de la Madeleine – original orange flower water was a syrup made from the blossoms of the Orangerie at the Palais de Versailles. Its calming effect must be somewhat psychological, a spoonful of it being all you need. The Maison Tanrade also has cherry, raspberry, currant, pineapple, lemon, orange and strawberry syrups for mixing soft drinks.

Spirits seem to be consumed in the largest quantities in places where the thermometer reaches levels that make the blood boil. Possibly this is because spirits have always been thought of as medicinal, killing all sorts of germs and microbes in the days before antibiotics took over.

The *Sundowner*, imbibed by many an old China Hand, Pukkah Sahib and other experts on Oriental Affairs, was meant to guard the unwary drinker against a sudden change in temperature. The recipe for this, in use for three hundred years I am told, is one part each of orange juice, lemon juice and curaçao to two parts of brandy, stirred vigorously with ice, and served in a largish cocktail glass. In South Africa they skip the curaçao and substitute Van der Hum instead.

In the sensual French Antilles, where the practice of magic is as normal as breathing, but where the pragmatically-minded Creoles pronounce that 'the fuller the pocketbook the better the girls like you', they also say that 'rum is truth', and after a few of their magical cold 'punches' you may agree. One such is *Euphoria*, which consists of two parts each of St James rum and grapefruit juice, one each of curaçao and pineapple juice, stirred with ice, and served in a large wine glass. It never fails to make me think of that strange sudden word 'nightfall' that so graphically describes the half hour when darkness drops and oppressively heated day becomes cool, polyphonic night in those latitudes.

From the steaming South to the literary North, my summer imagination skips to a Chekhov scene from almost any of his plays, though preferably perhaps *The Cherry Orchard*. As the characters plunge their inexorable ways into some new psychological maze, the low Russian summer sunlight glints on tall glasses of cold *Tea à la Russe*, with cherry preserve stirred into it, and sunk to the bottom of the glass. This drink is very refreshing, although it never seems to relieve Chekhov's gloom much. A small administration of vodka per glass might help a smile or two to reach your lips.

Exotic parts these days also include the unexplored, mysterious terrain of the American Middle West, as the natives go about their weekendly rite of plodding after a tiny white ball towards the nineteenth hole and relaxation. Once arrived at this fabled resting place, a common refresher is a Mint Julep (see page 32).

In Scandinavia, under the midnight sun, it is aquavit you drink in June

8

when all good Swedes, Norwegians, Danes and perhaps even Finns think it heretical not to eat *kraftor* (crayfish) on their outdoor porches with a napkin around their necks. After six of them it is imperative to take a huge schnapps. With this you get back into form for the next six, and so on. A true Scandinavian can go through a gross or two of crayfish, and quite a good deal of aquavit at a sitting. Other nationalities don't do too badly at it either, once they get the idea.

The ubiquitous Scandinavians have even invaded the New World with a mixture of Cherry Heering (which is Danish) with tequila. Known as a *Mexican Peter*, this combination is said to have rather interesting results when made with one part Danish and three parts Mexican, served on the rocks. The Danish part cools down the hot Mexican part for an almost perfect summer combination.

The Côte d'Azur, where all those lotus-eaters are now claiming not to be eating lotuses any more after the painful effects of inflation, is brought to mind by a *Perroquet*. This drink is sharp with the freshness of a dash of crème de menthe and cool with the anise taste of one part Pernod, plus five parts iced soda water.

Sometimes you can find pomegranate juice, imported in tins from Iran. If so, you can reproduce a Persian summer delight (as served by the Teheran Hilton) called a *Golnar*. This is a tall glass or silver goblet, with a measure of vodka (Persian of course), a dash of cherry brandy, and ice; fill with the pomegranate juice.

The whitest and most exotic summer drink I can remember had to do with a Pernod and water, taken on the quay of the Old Port in Marseille while the occupation troops were still not too far away, and the general euphoria of the French had not faded. I sat in the bar at the end of the Canebière feeling lonesome. I said 'a Pernod' but actually there must have been quite a few, for I managed eventually, in my bad French, to strike up an extremely friendly relationship with a good-looking young lady sitting beside me at the bar. The last thing I remember was saying goodbye to her as the cool dawn broke, and we were walking off in different directions, having wined and dined very well and settled various world problems – I still didn't even know her name.

As I watch the clear alcohol, be it Pernod, Ricard, ouzo, raki or whichever of those anise long drinks, with the ice clinking in them, turn milky, and the glittering Mediterranean stretching off into the Eleutherian haze, I still feel a wave of cool friendliness waft over me. Just right for holidays.

Summer drinks should be colourful: green for the cool look; yellow for the hot; red, blue, black, pink and rainbow for various moods. One way to keep yourself amused during a long hot summer is to mix your drinks in Technicolor.

Red ones are the easiest and most common because there are several red flavourings like cherry brandy, Dubonnet, grenadine, Byrrh and cassis. Cassis, by the way, is simply blackcurrants marinated in alcohol with sugar, so for a facsimile thereof, if you have none in the house, try currant syrup.

Dubonnet produces another shade of pinkness in a long cool drink. One hot Spanish summer I spent my time trying to match the colour of the Aigua Blava rocks with an accompanying drink. 'You and your pink rocks' is still a sort of battle cry among friends who were there at the time. The nearest I ever came to a match was a fizz made with two measures of Dubonnet, a teaspoon of cherry brandy, the juice of half an orange and a quarter of a lemon, shaken with ice, strained into a glass which I then filled with soda water.

Even simpler is a measure of Dubonnet, juice of half an orange, ice, shake, strain, serve; or half Dubonnet, half whisky, stirred with ice, served with a cherry. I happen to like ice in my drinks so I would serve all of these on the rocks, and remember that you can even make pink 'rocks' by sprinkling the water in your ice tray with angostura bitters before freezing.

A drink you can enjoy with summer meals, invented and long enjoyed by the Spanish, is a sort of red wine punch called *Sangria*. What is good about it is that its flavour does not pall because the taste changes with each new batch. You mix, in a large jug, equal parts – say a bottle each – of soda water and an inexpensive red wine. Add whatever fresh fruit you have in the house, sliced to let the juices escape; strawberries, raspberries, crushed currants, a sliver or two of orange or lemon or both. Stir in sugar to taste (about four teaspoons for this quantity) and let the mixture sit for an hour or so to blend the tastes. Fill with ice and serve. Some recipes call for added brandy, but that nullifies the nice lightness of the drink, I think.

Grenadine gives a drink the blush of innocence, though the innocence may be false. Like that of a French version of a tall cooler, *La Rose Americaine* – a measure of cognac, a dash of Pernod in a tall glass, two tablespoons of grenadine, plenty of ice and fill with barley water.

Coolers, by the way, are long, well-iced drinks, perfect for hot days, usually made with one of the basic alcohols (gin, vodka, whisky, rum) to which you add flavourings (sugar, lemon, the liqueur of your choice) and soda water. Since the vital ingredient of all coolers is 'coolth' remember this trick to make sure you get the most chilling experience. Glasses, drink and soda must all be chilled before mixing. So put drink, flavourings and ice – lots of it – in a tall glass and stir well to chill the whole mixture. Then only add the chilled soda, with a tiny swish of the spoon to mix. This keeps the sparkle which disappears fast if it is stirred too hard. Be sure to use a good sized glass, for the more it contains, the longer it will stay cold. And, like a wine glass, it should be filled to only about an inch from the rim.

Sometimes, as a different form of cooling, a *Cannonball* is fun. Shave and crush ice until it can be packed into balls. Drench the ice balls with a liqueur or even port or sherry and eat them as you would a sorbet.

If you have an eye for green there is a nice line in green concoctions too, with mint, green Chartreuse, lime and crème de menthe to dye them withal.

Yellow, when you're feeling blue will perhaps cheer you up. A *Yellow Parrot* of equal parts apricot brandy, yellow Chartreuse and Pernod is a short cooling concoction guaranteed to take your mind off the weather no matter what. Advocaat, a creamy liqueur made from yolks of eggs plus grape brandy (one of the least alcoholic of liqueurs), mixed with sparkling lemonade gives another good summer thirst quencher. Better still if it has a drop of kirsch added and a few ice cubes to freshen it up.

From yellow into the orange colour band is an easy switch with a Spanish favourite – orange juice in a tumbler with a measure of medium dry sherry added. This is even more eye-catching when shaken with the white of an egg to make it light and frothy. An *Orange Fizz* can be made either simply, with equal parts gin and orange juice, or with two parts gin, one of orange juice, and half each of lemon and lime juice. Both need shaking with ice, and a dash of Pernod, strain into a tumbler and fill with soda water.

An *In Drink* is an exotic number introduced by the Rolling Stones and consists of two measures of tequila in a tall glass with plenty of ice, topped up with fresh orange juice and a dash of grenadine, decorated with slices of orange and lemon and sipped through a straw.

But if you feel in need of something really potent, try a *Zombie*. Ideally, you need a measure each of light, medium and dark rums, one of lime juice, four drops of cherry brandy and four of apricot brandy. Shake well with ice, pour into a tall glass. Decorate with pineapple and cherry. If you have papaya juice and pineapple juice handy, substitute these for the quarter lime juice, but add the juice of one lime. You can also float a spoonful of demerara rum on the top of the whole business if you feel in the mood.

For a drink that will make you jump, mix three parts apricot brandy, one part lemon juice, stir with ice, strain into a glass – it's a *Hop Toad*.

Seldom, on a warm day, with your friends playing golf, tennis or cricket, is there a more refreshing drink to serve than a sparkling wine-based punch. Such a punch should look as summery as it tastes, and even the table it is on should be decorated with greenery and bright happy flowers. If you don't care much about the quality of the game, *Champagne Punch* (see page 86) is perfection. It makes you feel rather Great Gatsby and relaxed just to think about it.

Some Warming
Winter Drinks

Mulled Wine, Gluhwein, Zambucca, Buttered Rum,
Buttered Whisky, Egg Nog, Connoisseur's Milk Punch,
Orange Brulot, Un Grog, Stirrup Cup,
Extra Festive Champagne Punch, Christmas Terrine,
Polish Bigos, Beetroot Savoury

In the high and far-off times, when there were such things as witches and demons, one way to get rid of unwanted warlocks was to hold a colossal wassail party. Everyone, Druids and hoi polloi alike, had a marvellous time and the demons were successfully routed – possibly drowned – in the most agreeable way.

You may not realize, as the Christmas wassail slides down your eager throat, that you are continuing an ancient and honourable pagan tradition. All those dances until cock-crow, libations, mysteries of barley sheaves and new wine, animal sacrifices, and religious ecstasy were far more convivial than a cocktail party and more interesting. But the general purpose of these mid-winter saturnalia, both prehistoric and present-day, is the same – to rid oneself of the cold-weather blues.

The season is a long one, and the winter, of course, even longer, so here is a variety of recipes for cheering things up that you can experiment with progressively. There are drinks that glow, for example, and there are nourishing drinks. There are the sociable drinks and there are those that you can sit by the fire and enjoy all by yourself.

Drinks that glow put you into the right humour for the time of year. One of the best of these is *Mulled Wine*. This is simply a spiced wine, sweetened and served piping hot. It is the drink for the open fireplace, after coming home from skating or skiing.

If you have a log on the fire and the poker isn't covered with coal dust, use it to keep the wine heated. Let the poker get red hot and stick it into the mull from time to time, or just before pouring, to maintain the temperature. You shouldn't use your best crystal punch bowl for mulled wine, but something metal. The sizzle and steam are spectacular and add a certain old-time taste.

I learnt this method during the most memorable Christmas I have spent since the days when I expected Santa Claus to come down the chimney. This was in the heart of Wales. Our Welsh house party was snowed in for four days for all the world as if we were in Antarctica. The host was fortunately a providential and genial one, and we all helped to keep the fireplace supplied with wood we chopped ourselves. His cellar was well stocked with wines and his larder with all sorts of eatables including the right spices. Talk about glow! We had wine mulled by poker in a score of ways and we came away with the procedure deliciously fixed in our minds.

Mulled Wine is made by poker-warming a bottle of wine in a bowl into which you have poured a syrup made of the peel of a lemon and an orange, grated nutmeg, two sticks of cinnamon and six whole cloves boiled in a cup of water. Usually it is made with red wine, but I prefer white myself. You can also make the wine much stronger by adding a measure or two of cognac. Anyone who has been skiing knows this drink as *Gluhwein,* which started, I believe, in the Austrian Alps, but has now spread to delight après skiers in most winter resorts.

Another glowing libation is a *Zambucca,* an Italian concoction with a very slight liquorice flavour. You pour Zambucca liqueur into a tall liqueur glass and add three whole coffee beans – this seems to be the optimum number in Italy – which float on top. Then set the whole thing alight. When the flame dies out, the drink is ready to sip.

Buttered Rum is another hot drink and pretty vigorous too. You put a measure of rum and a teaspoonful of brown sugar in a tumbler and pour in hot water. Then float a small lump of butter on top, stirring until it is dissolved. Finally put in half a teaspoonful of mixed ground spices – cloves, allspice, mace, and a good bit of cinnamon or nutmeg. You can use cider instead of water for this drink, if you wish, and for the children cider only, omitting the rum.

A hot *Buttered Whisky* makes a pleasant alternative: two ounces of the best whisky, one ounce of fresh orange juice, and a teaspoon of sugar, in a tumbler or beer mug. Fill with hot water, stir and inhale. Add a half teaspoon of butter to float on top. Now drink and relax.

A good way to pick up a few reviving calories when you are feeling low is with egg-based drinks. Personally I find them a bit too filling, but sometimes on a crisp, cold New Year's Eve, they seem to suit the mood of the occasion perfectly. There are dozens of ways to make an *Egg Nog* and I am sure to get into trouble with some people over my recipe, but at least it has the quality of simplicity and can be either a one-man affair, or expanded to serve as many as you like. An individual portion consists of an egg, a teaspoonful of sugar, a tumblerful of milk, and a measure of almost any kind of drink you can name – sherry, port, Madeira, cognac, rum, whisky or Calvados will do. You shake the drink and the rest of the ingredients in cracked ice, pour into a tall glass, and sprinkle nutmeg on top.

When you make this egg nog for a group, however, it is best to take some care with the preparation of the eggs. The yolks should be beaten separately until frothy. Whip the sugar into them, add the drink gradually while stirring, then let the mixture stand for an hour. Now beat the whites until stiff and fold them into the mixture. Finally, egg nogs should be kept in the refrigerator. And don't put ice into them. Serve in a large punch bowl, after dusting the top with grated nutmeg.

Christmas and New Year are, if nothing else, times of extra sociability, and some of the most sociable drinks are the punches and champagne mixes. In one such holiday period, I travelled with a connoisseur of such things from New York to Buffalo for Christmas. We had hardly left the purlieus of Manhattan when a tremendous thirst took my friend and we stopped at the nearest pub for a *Milk Punch*. The barman was uninstructed in anything so complicated, and my friend took over. From then on, our progression was slow since we had to sample the techniques of every bar we passed along the route. I think it took us twenty-three hours to negotiate the passage. By the end of that time, we had reduced the recipe to its most basic form.

I pass on to you, for its historical value, the recipe achieved by trial and error on this unique trip. It is made with two measures of calvados in a cup of milk, with sugar to taste and not too much of that. These basic ingredients are shaken with cracked ice until thoroughly chilled, poured into a tumbler, and if you have the energy, dusted with nutmeg.

Of course you can turn basic milk punch into one of those nourishing drinks by adding an egg, or make it richer by using cream instead of milk. And if the weather is too cold for an iced drink, you can warm it up by using hot milk. But a punch is essentially a frappéed drink, to be served in a frosted glass, not just a cold drink like a highball.

Since the sages say 'presentation is one fourth of the pleasure of a drink', I suggest a complicated Creole creation for especially festive winter occasions. This bit of show-biz is called an *Orange Brulot*. You slice around the equator of an orange with a sharp knife, just deep enough to cut the skin, but not the fruit. With the handle of a spoon loosen the skin for about an inch above and below the cut, without tearing the peel. Carefully turn the skin inside out so that you have a kind of bowl at both ends, one up, one down. The down one forms the base, the up one the cup. You then put a lump of sugar and a measure of heated kirsch in the cup part. Turn down the lights, and at a signal have each guest light his own goblet and, with a teaspoon, stir to make the flames dance like fireworks. When the flame goes out, the brulot is ready to drink, and you or the children can eat the oranges after.

Un Grog is the French traditional pneumonia stopper: their version of the old British standby is made with a tot of rum, sugared to taste, in a tall glass liberally cut with hot water. If you like, you can add a lemon slice.

Traditions are often connected with special dates, and usually mid-winter ones at that. In Scotland on New Year's Eve, which they call Hogmanay for some obscure Celtic reason, the haggis is brought in to the skirl of pipes and helped down the revellers' gullets with doses of the local wine – Scotch whisky. The Swedes celebrate December 13 as Santa Lucia's Day with candles dangerously burning in crowns on the girls' heads, and the Scandinavian firewater, aquavit, burning deliciously in the celebrants' tummies. On Chinese New Year, which might be any day in January or February because their calendar is based on moon movements, the thing to have is a Mai Tai – the rice wine that is the traditional toast of Peking.

Hunting has spawned some traditions of its own, not the least of which is the *Stirrup Cup*. This used to be a simple glass of wine or brandy taken as you sat in your saddle before yoicking and tallyho-ing off over the countryside. But George Washington is said to have invented a more complicated way to start the hunt off, which required a jigger of cherry brandy, one of cognac, and the juice of half a lemon.

Champagne Punch probably has the most glamorous associations of any Christmas-time drink. Just the idea of making it conjures up euphoric feelings, and the thought of using the most aristocratic of wines in this plebeian way adds to the sensation of open-handedness that the season seems to require. There are many recipes for *Champagne Punch* but one of the best is a sort of huge champagne cocktail.

For this you need the juice of two lemons and an orange, four measures of cognac and two bottles of champagne. A small amount of sugar, say about four teaspoonfuls, should be dampened with orange bitters. Put this with the fruit juices and cognac into a large bowl, making sure the sugar is dissolved. Then add a large lump of ice, and just before serving pour in the champagne and stir. This should serve ten to twelve people.

Finally, of course, without any fuss, apart from popping the corks, you can have a perfect fiesta with perfectly plain champagne. Just chill the bottles, nudge out the corks, and pour.

All over the world the most serious winter drinking – and feasting – is done at Christmas time. The Austrians surprisingly serve fish. A typical holiday meal might start with a fried carp, potato salad and baked mushrooms, though they tend to choose roast goose. Stuffed with sauerkraut and additionally flavoured by basting with white wine, this makes a delicious Christmas dish. In France Christmas is essentially a family affair. People tend to give presents they have made themselves. One friend of mine, for example, makes a *Christmas Terrine* of anchovies for her friends. She uses two pounds of salted anchovies, thoroughly washed in running water, and de-boned. These are put in a bowl, covered with a pint of milk and left for exactly two hours. Then into a colander, rinsed with water and dried by patting with paper towels. Chop four or five cloves of garlic (or two fat shallots) together with a handful of parsley. Lay out the anchovy fillets in layers in a terrine and cover each layer with the parsley-garlic mixture. Cover the whole dish with vegetable oil and leave to macerate for forty-eight hours at room temperature. Keep in the refrigerator for a week before eating on country style bread. It will keep at least a month in the fridge.

In Poland animals are said to acquire human voices on Christmas Eve which could be somewhat upsetting if you weren't prepared for it. There the traditional Christmas dish is *Bigos* washed down with quantities of Polish vodka. In a large pot place two pounds (900 g) of sauerkraut, two bay leaves and a little boiling water. Boil one and a half pounds (675 g) of cabbage in another large pot until tender. Soak two large dried mushrooms in water, clean, and cook until tender, then cut into strips and add to the cabbage. Wash six ounces (175 g) of lean pork, dry and fry, sprinkled with salt, until brown. Cool and cut into thin strips and add, with four ounces (125 g) of bacon, to sauerkraut and simmer until tender. Fry a sliced onion in lard and add to the cabbage. Mix the cabbage and sauerkraut. Add half a pound (225 g) of smoked ham, cut in strips, quarter of a pound (125 g) of Polish sausage, skinned and sliced, two ounces (50 g) of tomato purée and a cup of red wine. Season with salt and pepper. Bring to the boil and cook gently for one and a half hours. Cool and leave in refrigerator for twenty-four hours. The more times this dish is reheated the tastier it gets.

Now, for perfect enjoyment of all these dishes, there must be liquid to wash them down. With the bigos, of course, you should serve vodka. In America you would doubtless be given an Old Fashioned before Christmas dinner. (See page 33.) In Austria or Germany you might be served a 'Kalte Ente' (cold duck) which consists of a bottle of champagne, two bottles of Moselle, half a bottle of soda water and the peel of a lemon which has been marinated for five minutes in the wine. Ice and serve.

One Warm Welsh Christmas

Seldom does any particular Christmas stand out in one's mind – at least not in mine. But a Christmas in Cymru – known to the majority of underpoetic, undermusical and underprivileged mortals as Wales, I shall never forget.

The invitation was to a place called Rhayader in the hilly heart of Wales and a rambling old homestead whose name was Rhydoldog (everything in Wales has either five 'l's' in it or an 'rh') familiarly nicknamed 'The Dog'. It belonged to Oonah, a lady with an apparently acidulous attitude towards Christmas but actually one of the kindest, most generous hostesses I've known.

'The Frenzied Feast' she calls it, claiming she'd like to go away where there is no Christmas, send no presents, hear no carols, turn Moslem and fast until the 'whole ghastly affair is over and it's safe to come back'. She also claims, contrarily, that she goes nowhere, spends more than she can afford, doesn't have time to become a convert, and 'bastes and bakes and bickers and boozes' the holiday away, hoping for at least some measure of peace and goodwill by keeping her guests at the television, turned up loud, for the whole dangerous three-day period.

The truth is both she and her guests love the performance and their pleasure in her style of hostessing is in no degree diminished by huge and continuous helpings of food and drink.

On Christmas Eve, for instance, the local choir singers appeared at the door to give us a song in the snow. Oonah's husband handed out bottles of beer as their reward. The catch was she had neglected to warn him she had filled those bottles with sloe gin. The choir sang 'Bless this House' to an unusually receptive audience. There was not a dry eye in the houseparty, nor a dry chorister able to wend his way back to Rhayader.

Later a group of urchins on the same mission showed up and were given the traditional sixpence each for their pains. Possibly because inflation had already set in, they objected to this and showed their displeasure by stuffing old newspapers into the ends of the drainpipes and setting them alight. This, as the little devils knew it would, caused a great roaring in the pipes, to the consternation of the household which, convinced that a tornado had struck, rushed out into the snow to the sniggers of the wassailers as they ran off.

Winters may be mild, but since in England one refuses to admit that it ever gets cold, you can easily freeze to death in a country house if the temperature drops – and it did. Except for the Yellow Drawing Room where a crackling log fire kept things slightly above freezing, the Red, Mauve and Blue rooms, to say nothing of the bedrooms, suffered from the fact that Grandfather had installed 'central heating' so specifically central that it neglected to extend beyond or above the hall. In the Yellow Drawing Room which was the centre of conviviality, Oonah's psychologically inspired décor framed the view to the valley through big windows with curtains fashioned from her mother's damask tablecloths – dyed a warming gold.

In that bow window, we eventually planted a thick-leaved Christmas tree, fresh and aromatic, hacked down on the property itself by a delegation of guests and host; spurred on by a ceremony that was half cocktail party, half pagan rite. Once installed, the tree was decorated traditionally, but gifts were handed out on Christmas Eve, leaving Christmas itself free for church and dinner. Church was to be somewhat confusing with children singing 'While shepherds washed their socks by night' but dinner was thoroughly organized. It began with leek soup. Choice of the leek as the official flower of Wales may be a relic of the Roman occupation armies. All Romans, it appears, thought leeks excellent for maintaining a sonorous voice. And the Welsh not only love to talk and make speeches, but seem to spend most of their time singing. So the mellifluous leek is important.

This is sometimes hard on friends, as is implied by the sixteenth-century Welshman who advised, 'If leekes you like but do their smelle dislike, eat onyons and you shall not smelle the leekes. If you of onyons would the scents expell, eat garlicke that shall downe the onyon's smell.'

After soup came a potato-fattened goose baked in the old brick oven. Logs were fired amid the bricks and the oven's heat tested by throwing a handful of flour in. When the flying flour browned as it was thrown in, the oven was cleared of wood, the bird stuffed with sage and onion, thrust in and left to cook until ready.

Rhydoldog geese were always fed on potatoes for a week or two before they were sacrificed for the Christmas feast. The tenant farmer brought them to the house ready dressed in 'waistcoats' of holly leaves, with red holly berries marching down the centre of their chests like buttons. After baking they were redecorated and brought to the table resplendent and tasting as good as they looked.

Vegetables included potato scooped out of its baked jacket, mixed with cheese and butter and replaced in the skin, and Brussels sprouts – 'Just a way of conveying water to the table,' as one of Oonah's less complimentary guests once said.

But this gastronomic gaffe was recouped with a complicated savoury – toast cut into a circle big enough to hold a round of beetroot. On this would be curled an anchovy. In the centre of the anchovy a dollop of thick cream was topped by a sprig of parsley. Dessert was traditional plum pudding, and mince pies almost afloat with brandy. On Boxing Day, the leftover goose became a fricassée, and the plum pudding was fried and served with cream.

The drinks at oldtime Rhydoldog Christmas dinners were segregated. The men got whisky served in individual decanters at each place, the ladies got wine. In our day there was such a profusion of whisky, wine, port and brandy that you could take your choice.

Oonah invented ways to get food into us without seriously interfering with other activities. One method was via a sort of Welsh version of Bœuf Bourguignonne, chunks of prime beef dunked in a mixture of hot oil and butter then dipped into various Welsh condiments. Another was Welsh Rarebit, a fine way to make a meal out of a piece of cheese and an egg, or a Swiss fondue with four mixed cheeses. All this washed down with a great deal of champagne and whisky, or wine.

The perfect ending to a Welsh Christmas from the point of us house-party guests was that a blizzard set in, and we were snowbound for four days.

We staggered back to London for a rest, exhausted but unforgettably happy.

What's Brewing?

Homemade Beer, Broodje, Danish Beer Soup,
Carp in Beer, Sauerkraut in Beer

Tony, an adventurous friend of mine, before taking off round the world in a Land Rover had the foresight to leave me the formula that inspired him to take the trip – a recipe for homemade beer. It has a distinguished parentage, for he got it from Sir Walter Scott, a descendant of the great novelist, and a neighbour of Tony.

Whether or not you plan to become a brewer or writer or even to make an expedition, I feel it essential that you should have an opportunity to try this inspirational beverage, so here is what you must do:

Put three pounds (1·4 kg) of malt extract, two ounces (50 g) of hops wrapped in muslin, half a teaspoonful of salt, and nine pounds (4 kg) of dark brown sugar into a gallon (4·5 l) of water. Bring this to a boil but watch it like a hawk for, at this point, just as your back is turned, it tends to boil over in a flash, like milk. My world-travelling friend's first try did this, and covered the kitchen floor with 'toffee', filled the house with a strong smell of burnt sugar and hops, a potent smell at best, and solidly sealed the stove doors – in fact, it was a mess. But it was not the end of the beer. Each home brewing is a unique artistic experience anyway, so what was left turned out fine.

If you catch the boiling point in time, turn down the heat and simmer for thirty-five minutes. Then add another two ounces (50 g) of hops, loose, and bring the liquid to the boil for another five minutes. Pour that into four and a half gallons (20 l) of cold water, allow it to cool to about seventy degrees, add a quarter of a pound (125 g) of dry yeast, strain out the hops and let the whole thing sit and ferment.

After a week or ten days the beer will have stopped fermenting and then you can bottle it. Into each bottle (and don't use square ones, they are too weak at the corners to hold the pressure) put a bit of sugar (Sir Walter's recipe says one teaspoonful per pint, but I think that makes the beer too sweet) to help develop the beer's 'head'. Siphoning is the easiest way to get the beer from the vat or tub into the bottles, but a mouthful of un-aged beer is nearly as unpleasant as one of petrol, so be wary. Let it age in the bottle at least two weeks – the flavour is even better after four.

A pretty sensational way to drink this, once it is ready, is to mull it. The poet Robert Southey describes how an aristocratic friend, Sir George Howland Beaumont, did this. He had a set of silver cups brought to the table, red hot. Into them the cold beer was poured with spectacular results. Southey recounts that 'it alarmed the guests to pick up the cups', but it seems the beer foamed over and cooled them almost immediately.

The most marvellous thing about beer to me is its smell – the aroma that permeates the brewery, that wafts through the bierhalle or the pub or the bar, that caresses your nostrils as you lift a foamy mug to suck in the first sip of the evening. It is indescribably a blend of malt and hops and yeast and warmth and friendliness. It makes you feel good all over!

Up in Vermont, one summer, as a boy, I worked as an extra hand on a farm. Three things I remember about that tough summer of hard hay pitching are: Mrs Hoisington's superb doughnuts, fresh from the clean deep fat; the Saturday night baths in the tin tub in the communal kitchen, and the lovely smell of the homebrew that spilled out of the tubs she made it in for the delectation and sustenance of the husky hired hands. I hope she's still at it and they still are enjoying it.

But there is a lot besides its aroma to recommend beer, including the fact that people have been drinking it for ever. Brewing has hardly changed since it was first invented. The secret was known to the Assyrians and the Pharoahs. The Egyptian *Book of the Dead* indicates that a form of barley brew was drunk as long ago as 3000 BC. Queen Elizabeth I was a fan, long before Women's Lib, and according to her chief minister, her beer was 'so strong as there is no man able to drink it'.

A rabbinical tradition, too, says the Hebrews in captivity in Babylon drank stuff called 'bre', which may be the origin of our word 'beer', as a magic protection from dread disease. The German tribes at war with Rome supposedly preserved their beer with hops, and their morale with the beer.

Beer, for those of us who like to know a fact or two about it, is made as it always has been from an infusion of malted barley – or in fact, almost any starchy cereal – flavoured with hops and fermented by yeast. Different processes or ingredients have led to different names for it. A malt drink the ancient Britons borrowed from their Norse invaders as 'ol' became 'ale', which was in those days a sweet fermented barley beverage, laced with honey.

Even before that, the Saxons were using hops to flavour their 'bier' and give it a dry bitterish quality. American beer is usually what is called 'lager' type, a German name describing a beer that is stored in vats (*lager* means warehouse, in German). This is a delicately aromatic, lightly hopped, creamy headed beer. Some of the best-known brands in the US are made where there is a concentration of descendants of German immigrants.

Americans, and most Europeans, like to drink beer cold, but the British like it at room temperature. In England, there is also 'old ale' that has been long aged and is dark, mellow, and smooth. The Scots prefer it this way. Pilsner, like lager, is a 'bottom fermented' beer. The yeast used for fermentation is introduced from the bottom of the vats and seeps upwards.

What most of us think of as an Irish monopoly, stout – just to show how international the drink is – got its name from the old French *estout*, meaning strong, which it is – strong, black and flavoured with roasted malt and barley.

Before I knew what a potent beverage beer could be, I spent a summer touring Germany. In my strange mixed 'native' costume of lederhosen, and black-and-white 'co-respondent's' shoes, I visited the Hofbraühaus in Munich, where I sat at one of the huge tables in the topmost room, an enormous functional palace devoted almost entirely to the delights of drinking beer from litre mugs. The celebrants would make an occasional pass at some food just to keep up appearances. My back was to one end of the hall where there was an innocent looking balcony overlooking the crowd.

About halfway through my fourth litre I was galvanized into involuntary action by a racket that caused me to jump about three feet from my bench. The brass band had sneaked into the balcony, and their opening 'oompah' was what did it. After that I understood what it meant to 'face the music', at least in Germany. Unnerved, my fifth litre did me in, and a kind German friend had to escort me home.

The British drink an incredible 27 Imperial gallons of beer per capita each year, only $1\frac{1}{2}$ gallons less than the Germans. The Americans drink a good deal, too – $26\frac{1}{2}$ American gallons (which are one-fifth less). The Danes claim to have the biggest brewery in the world, and they drink beer at all times for any reason at all. A French savant, Dr Edouard de Pomiane, says 'beer is the most scientific of all alcoholic drinks' which is perhaps not the best reason for drinking it! And it is true that modern breweries look more like science labs than anything else.

For centuries, however, brewing was more of an art in which luck and skill supplemented theory. A bad fermentation was said to be caused by such things as (Women's Lib-ers, this is not my diagnosis) a woman walking through the fermentation room. Today, a tiny detail change in manufacture is enough to give the brew a special flavour, and pasteurization has almost eliminated chance. The Belgians, for instance, let their yeastless beer age in bottles, where it undergoes a second fermentation. This stuff, called by them *geuse lambic*, is acid tasting to most palates, but has many a devotee. The Russians make beer from oats and something called kvass from rye bread. And Japanese sake is really beer made from rice, but Kirin or Suntory beer is delicious, despite a strange label announcing it as 'fresh real draft'!

In Holland, where there is also a huge beer industry, they ran into trouble because of an apparently public spirited policy. Heineken's brewery in Amsterdam allowed visitors to down as much beer as they liked while watching the brewing process. Such queues of thirsty hippies filled the nearby streets, like people waiting for a cinema seat, they had to limit their generosity. If you are not that thirsty but need a quick lunch, try making a *Broodje*. Take a soft white roll, split and butter it, and pile it high with herrings or fresh-from-the-sea shrimps, the way the Dutch do. Two *broodjes* washed down with a glass of golden Dutch beer will keep you going till dinner time.

If you are still hungry, a *Danish Beer Soup* may be in order. For this you need a pint (6 dl) of dark malt beer or ale, eight slices of dark rye bread or pumpernickel, one cup of water, the grated rind and juice of a lemon, sugar and cream. Break the bread into small pieces in a deep dish. Mix in the beer and water and allow this to soak for three to eight hours. Simmer until it thickens and then either strain or purée it. Stir in the lemon rind and juice, sweeten to taste, and bring it to the boil. Serve hot with cream.

A carp cooked in beer is a French delicacy. You need two finely chopped onions, lightly sautéed in butter until they are translucent. Spread them in a deep dish, adding thyme, a bay leaf, a finely chopped piece of celery, several grains of freshly ground black pepper, a clove, and three ounces of diced gingerbread. Fillet the carp, salt and pepper it, and put it on the bed of herbs you have made. Then pour in enough pale beer or ale to cover the fish. Poach it in the oven at low heat, about 300–350 degrees F (150–80 C, gas mark 2–4), for about twenty-five minutes. If the carp has roe, take it out and poach separately in salted water with a dash of lemon juice. Place carp fillets on a heated serving dish, and garnish with the roe. Sieve the cooking juices, reduce them by half, add a bit of butter, and pour over the fish. Serve hot.

Of course, sauerkraut, simmered in beer, is a classic. For this you wash half a pound of sauerkraut per person under cold running water. Place it in a pot and cover it with beer, then cover the pot and simmer very slowly for three or four hours until it is the consistency you like, crisp or soft. Some add a slice of salt pork or bacon, in the bottom of the pot, plus a finely chopped garlic clove and a few twists of the pepper-mill before cooking. Garnish is usually knackwurst, pork sausages, roast pork loin, bacon and potatoes, cooked separately, but served with the sauerkraut, and with French mustard.

Bottled beer hates sunlight and if it is bounced around too much before serving, it not only loses flavour, but, because it spurts on opening, is wasteful. The proper way to pour beer from bottle or tin is into a tipped glass for the first half-glassful, then to straighten up the glass for the rest so that a head will form.

Philosophically speaking, beer is a drink people love to the tune of some forty-three billion glasses full – or emptied – per year. So I leave you with this 'thought' as set forth in a bit of anonymous verse discovered by a beer drinker friend in a Somerset beer emporium:

> The horse and mule live thirty years
> And nothing know of wines and beers.
> The goat and sheep at twenty die
> And never taste a scotch or rye.
> The cow drinks water by the ton
> And at eighteen is mostly done.
> The dog at fifteen cashes in
> Without the aid of rum and gin.
> The cat in milk and water soaks
> And then in twelve short years it croaks.
> The modest, sober, bone-dry hen
> Lays eggs for nogs and dies at ten.
> All animals are strictly dry
> But sinful, ginful, beer-soaked men
> Survive for three-score years and ten,
> While some of them, a very few,
> Stay pickled till they're ninety-two.

Inside Cider

Ham Baked in Cider, Chicken with Cider Sauce,
Winter Mull, Spiced Cider, Calvados Cup,
Cider Sparkle, Cider Punches, Paradise,
Four-Man Cider Cup, Mulled Cider,
Cider Soup, Cider-Apple Sauce

When I was a schoolboy, making hard cider (that is alcoholic cider) out of apple juice, it never occurred to me that I was using a magic fruit, sacred to Venus, the lure with which Wisdom, represented by a spotless virgin, got the Unicorn, symbol of purity, to lay its head in her lap. Nor did I know that King Arthur went to the secret Island of Apple Trees to be healed of a near-mortal wound. Nor again that the apple tree itself is the tree of immortality-through-wisdom.

My motives were less mystical. The idea was simply to find something drinkably alcoholic. And the easiest thing then was to buy a gallon jug of cider from the nearest farm, and hang this jug, discreetly disguised so the masters wouldn't find it, out of my dormitory window. In the icy nights of New England, with temperatures sometimes down to twenty degrees below, the cider would freeze, leaving in the centre of the jug a small, but interesting, core of 'applejack'. This was the tipple of a selected few companions, surreptitiously sipped, and deliciously illegal.

Today the commercial cider makers of this world tend to look down their noses at small-scale cider making as 'an affair of the farms', of untrustworthy quality. But that natural, undependable cider, allowed to ferment until it became quite alcoholic, without distilling or freezing was and still is, if you can find it, a wonderfully agreeable drink. A sip of it gives you the very essence of apples and apples, one should not forget, were considered sacred by the Greeks who had observed that cut in half, cross-wise, the core of each half makes a five-pointed star, emblem of immortality!

But neither this nor its heady connection with Aphrodite, the goddess of love, has rubbed off on apple cider which although a true wine – if wine is defined as the product of fermenting fruit juice – has a low alcoholic content and has never caught on as a drink for lovers.

In fact there are few references to cider in early Mediterranean literature which probably means that, even with its divine testimonial, cider-making was never as easy as winemaking.

In the old days cider used to be difficult to store and transport. Pasteurization and modern bottling have overcome that minor inconvenience. Like other wines, cider tastes range from dry to quite sweet, and there is a naturally sparkling version of it, too. It even comes in draught form, served like beer from a keg.

It can also be made from any kind of apple juice, but the best comes from apples that have a lot of acid and tannin which makes them sour and bitter for eating. Like a good deal of wine, cider is made uniform in quality by blending. The fruit is squashed into a pulp, called pomace, then pressed immediately into juice. The entire process is speedy—from the whole fruit to filtered juice in vats takes less than half an hour. For the driest cider, fermentation is allowed to go on until it is complete. For a sweeter version the fermentation is stopped before completion. Cider's alcoholic content varies from three to seven per cent, between that of beer and of wine, and some is allowed to ferment twice, to produce a sparkling drink vaguely like champagne.

Cider can become the raw material for apple brandy – calvados, as the French call it, or applejack in America. A good calvados is as mellow and smooth as a fine cognac. Applejack tends to be more amateurly made in clandestine stills, but a well-matured one is a wonderfully satisfying after-dinner drink. It used to be possible in France to have your apple cider turned into brandy by travelling stills, the *bouilleurs de crus*, so you could have your own apple brandy. This pleasant facility has been abolished in a postwar wave of puritanism.

King Charlemagne, turning his talents to advertising, was possibly the first man to have actively promoted cider. Among the laws he introduced were some which advised his subjects to drink cider and to share their secret cooking recipes. He probably realized it was a great thirst quencher, blending best with 'peasant' food, coarse, simple dishes, salads and cold meals.

There is quite a tradition of cookery with cider. For example, it produces a lovely subtle flavour if you add it to the water in which a ham is boiled. There is also a delicious New England dish of *Ham Baked in Cider*. To make this you soak the ham in cider overnight, bake in medium oven (twenty minutes per pound), and baste occasionally with cider. Remove from oven, strip off the skin, spread the ham with brown sugar, mustard and crumbs, and stud with cloves. Return to oven for half an hour to glaze, basting occasionally with cider.

Chicken, too, is good with cider sauce. In a deep pan, sauté six chicken legs, salted, peppered, and dusted with flour, in butter until golden. Stir in one pint (6 dl) of dry cider, bring to the boil, then add one whole onion, and simmer for about forty minutes. Remove the onion, stir in one-quarter pint of cream, cooking gently for one minute until the sauce is smooth. Serve with a sprinkle of parsley, and lemon quarters.

Cider also goes well with fish and shellfish and with pork and can be used instead of wine in most recipes that call for white wine. But beware of adding cider to any dish being cooked in an iron pot. The iron tends to turn the cider black.

Cider drinks begin with *Winter Mull* made with a cup of cider, a dash of bitters, a splash of rum or calvados if you have it, three cloves, a small piece of cinnamon, a twist of lemon peel, one teaspoon of powdered sugar and a pinch of allspice, combined in a saucepan and heated but not boiled. Pour into a tall glass.

Another good winter drink is *Spiced Cider* which has the added advantage of being low in calories: heat a quart of dry cider with one cinnamon stick or a pinch or two of cinnamon powder, five cloves, a pinch each of nutmeg and mace, five thin lemon slices. Simmer for half an hour. Non-dieters can add a measure of dark rum per glass.

Equally good as a summer drink is a *Calvados Cup*. For this take a quart (1·1 l) of cider, a measure each of Calvados, cognac and curaçao and mix with a pint (6 dl) of soda water in a jug with ice cubes and two large sprigs of mint.

Festive occasions call for a *Cider Sparkle*. In a glass jug mix a quarter pint (1·5 dl) each of lemon juice and gin, and five tablespoons of honey. Just before serving, add six to eight cubes of ice and stir in one bottle of champagne cider. Remove the ice and serve in wine glasses, garnished with slim slices of cucumber.

Cider Punch makes a good summer drink. There are various versions of this but one that I particularly like is a mixture of a bottle of dry cider or apfelsaft, a pound (450 g) or more of ripe strawberries and the juice of two oranges. After washing the berries and slicing them, soak them in the orange juice for an hour. Pour in the cider, stir and serve. When the liquid has been drunk, the berries are marvellous with cream. Another variation uses a bottle of dry cider, one to one and a half pounds (450–675 g) of ripe strawberries and the juice of two oranges. Cut the berries in half and soak them in the orange juice, for at least an hour, in a large pitcher. Then pour in the cider, ice enough to cool the drink, and serve.

Slightly stronger is a *Paradise* for which you steep a pound (450 g) of strawberries, sliced peaches or almost any soft fruit, with two jiggers of cognac and two quarts (2·2 l) of cider for at least an hour. Add sugar to taste and ice, and just before serving pour in a bottle of soda water or sparkling wine.

The Clermont Club in London used to serve a *Four-Man Cider Cup* using a quart (1·1 l) of cider, a wine glass of maraschino, another of curaçao and a third of brandy. Put all of these in a three-pint jug with ice and a little soda water. Stir and pour into a tall glass with slices of fruit and a sprig of mint to decorate.

Most mulls, usually made with port or red wine, can also be made with cider; put a teaspoon of tea leaves, four or five cloves, half a teaspoon of powdered cinnamon and a pinch of grated lemon peel in a large tub with one and three-quarter pints (1 l) of boiling water, which you allow to sit for five minutes. Meantime, heat a bottle of apple wine or cider gently, with a wine-glassful of rum and some sugar if you like. Strain the tea mixture into the punch bowl. Add the cider and rum and serve hot.

In the old days, punch, was a sociable drink and patrons of the pubs used to mix their own recipes as they sat round a table and gossiped. Drinking some of them could be a befuddling experience. Robert Smith Surtees (in his book *Handley Cross*) describes what happened, after a night of brandy punch drinking, to his hero Jorrocks and his pal Pigg. Jorrocks speaks first: "'Look out of the winder, James, and see wot sort of a night it is." James staggered up, and after a momentary grope about the room – for they were sitting without candles – exclaimed, "Hellish dark and smells of cheese." "Smells of cheese!" repeated Mr Jorrocks, looking round, "Man, you've got your nob in the cupboard."'

A cider punch may prove less drastic. Why not try this version and see? Put four ounces (125 g) of sugar, one quart (1·1 l) each of water and cider, the juice of two oranges and three lemons, plus four cloves, into a large pan and heat slowly to boiling point. Remove from heat, add an eighth of a bottle each of rum, Bols apricot brandy and cognac and stir well. Pour into a punch bowl and decorate with slices of lemon, orange and grated nutmeg.

For still another variation mix a one-litre bottle of dry cider and two bottles of dry white wine in a large punch bowl into which you have dropped the peeled skin of a whole lemon, and the sliced meat of same. Add a glass of vodka and five slices of fresh pineapple, cut into bites. A block of ice. Serve with fresh mint.

Something entirely different is *Cider Soup* – an old European favourite. Bring three litres of cider slowly to a boil, stir in a third of a cup of brown sugar. Keep it hot while you brown three handfuls of stale, cubed bread in butter (about three tablespoons of it) and season with salt and pepper. Beat three whole eggs, and add two tablespoons of sugar and a cup of cream mixed with two tablespoons of flour to them as you beat. Add to that three tablespoons of dark rum, a few grains of allspice, and pour this mixture into the warm cider, still beating away. Sprinkle the croûtons over the soup and serve.

And finally, always remember that apple sauce made with cider instead of water is delicious.

How to be Happy but Temperate

Clam Juice Cocktail, Angostura Highball,
Mexican Coffee, Redcurrant Punch, Redcurrant Cooler,
Karkade, Chufa, Citron Pressé,
Chilled Elderflower, Chocolate Malted Milk,
Black Cow, Apple Punch, Lebanese Cinnamon Tea,
Barley Water, Avocado Ade, Iranian Yoghurt Cocktail,
Kibbutz Fruit Cocktail, Dump Punch, Lemonale,
Mock Champagne, Strawberry Punch, Lemonade,
Tunisian Freshener, Tomato Cocktail,
Non-Alcoholic Wine

Whether we like it or not, we are all walking around with ·003 per cent of alcohol in our bloodstreams at every hour of the day. Nevertheless, the sad truth is that in the lives of most of us there will be times when the joys of adding to that percentage pall. The problem then is what to do with your drinking hand while everyone else is downing that third cocktail, or the last scotch, or simply when you have a guest who thirsts for something cool, refreshing but non-alcoholic.

One answer to the first question might be a drink I used to serve to my straitlaced deaconess aunt while others drank martinis – *Clam Juice Cocktail*. In it, three tablespoons of lemon juice, two of tomato ketchup, three cups of clam juice (which may be obtained in tins) plus, optionally, a teaspoon of grated celery and half a teaspoon of grated onion, a drop of Tabasco and perhaps salt, are combined, chilled, strained, and happily downed, without harming anyone's scruples about alcohol.

For those who are not allowed to take any alcohol and wish that they were, a drink that tastes as though it might have some alcohol in it is an *Angostura Highball*. This is simply ginger ale and a teaspoonful of angostura bitters in a tall glass with ice. Of course, you can make this alcoholic by adding gin or vodka.

If it's 'trompe l'œuil' you need – some way to disguise teetotalism at a party – the Mexicans have a drink that could pass for Irish Coffee. It is a wine glass of coffee mixed with a tablespoon of orange juice and a teaspoon of lemon juice, on top of which you float whipped cream.

Actually, in India where alcoholic drinks are prohibited, the almost universal accompaniment to all meals is a lime juice ade. It is not too sweet, yet it adds a tartness to plain water that pleased my palate. In India it is made with fresh limes, which the Indians insist are an active digestive agent, and should be used generously.

A young lady of twelve of my acquaintance tells me that a combination of concentrated redcurrant juice and lime juice in equal amounts, cut with soda water, makes an excellent punch, and the quantity she imbibes seems to bear out her diagnosis. She is also very favourably inclined toward another exotic drink – mango juice from tinned mangos, taken straight but chilled.

The late Lady Penrose, a fabulous hostess and cook, gave her occasional temperate guest a *Redcurrant Cooler*. This needs a syrup made of two cups of water, one cup of sugar, into which two cups of redcurrant juice are stirred, then six tablespoons of frozen orange concentrate, a quarter cup of lemon juice and half a tablespoon of almond extract. This is chilled and just before serving you add two cups of dry ginger ale.

Her own favourite hot weather concoction was a *Karkade*: it is made with hibiscus flowers – you can get them dried in fancy food stores or in herb and spice emporia. Wash a handful of the flowers and put them in a pint of cold water with two tablespoons sugar. Bring to the boil and simmer for ten minutes. The syrup is strained and kept in the refrigerator for use as flavouring in drinks, or simply diluted with soda water and ice and drunk as you might lemonade. The Spaniards often drink a brew called *Chufa*. This is made with tiger nuts but almonds or hazel nuts would do. Pour a quarter of a pound (125 g) of nuts (tiger nuts need soaking overnight) in a blender with a quarter of a pint (1·5 dl) of water, and grind as fine as possible. Add a teaspoon of sugar. Strain, cool, or add ice cubes and it's ready.

The French, in their more abstemious moods, are inclined to favour various infusions of herbs or flowers. An infusion is simply made by steeping herbs or flowers in boiling water or milk until the flavours are passed into the liquid. Vanilla, lemon or orange rind all give good steeped flavours. The flowers of the lime tree dried and steeped in boiling water are popular for their soothing qualities even today, but back in the Middle Ages lemonade was the French passion, and *limonadier* was the name for sellers of non-alcoholic drinks of all kinds. A *Citron Pressé* – the juice of a lemon, in a glass with ice, a bowl of sugar to use as you like, and soda to lengthen the drink – is still a popular drink on a hot day in any French sidewalk café.

An old English idea was an infusion of nettles. The dried blossoms of white nettles were steeped to make 'juice'.

> If they'd drink nettles in March
> And eat mugwort in May,
> So many fine maidens
> Wouldn't go to the clay

was the plaintive song of one Michael Denham only one hundred years ago.

You have to be careful with milk because it is more food than drink but a delicious drink is made by simmering a quart (1·1 l) of milk with a cup of elderflowers. Beat two egg yolks with half a cup of sugar and add to the milk after straining out the flowers. Beat the egg whites very stiff and mix in. Chill and serve with a dash of cinnamon or nutmeg. In the States a favourite of the younger set is *Chocolate Malted Milk*. You whirl a tumblerful of milk, a scoop or spoonful of chocolate ice cream, a tablespoon of chocolate syrup and two of powdered malt in a blender (or whip it with an eggbeater) until smooth. Add another scoop of ice cream, if you can stand it, and serve with a straw. If you want to make a meal of it, add a raw egg!

Another American idea is the *Black Cow*, which consists of two spoonfuls of vanilla ice cream in a tall glass, filled then to the top with coke. Stir and sip.

Cider or apple juice as punch, makes another good summer drink. I like a mixture of a bottle of dry cider or apfelsaft, a pound (450 g) or more of ripe strawberries and the juice of two oranges. After washing the berries and slicing them, soak them in the orange juice for an hour. Pour in the cider, stir and serve. When the liquid is drunk eat the berries with cream.

Normally accustomed to slaking parched gullets in the deserts, the Lebanese have a hot anise drink for the colder days. Four teaspoons of aniseed and one of cinnamon powder are boiled for three minutes in four cups of water. This is poured into teacups and sugar added to taste with a sprinkling of chopped walnuts and almonds.

Vegetable juices can easily be extracted with the right blender attachments. The best for 'straight' drinking are celery and carrot juices. Use the outside stalks of celery since they have a stronger taste and the hearts are good to munch separately. Just thrust as many of either vegetable as you like into the blender and let it reduce them to juice, strain, add a drop of Worcestershire sauce to give it a wallop. A drop or two of orange juice in the carrot version will keep its colour.

When I was a child, old-fashioned remedies for colliwobbles were still in use. One medicinal but pleasant drink was *Barley Water* for upset stomachs and a generally calming effect. This was made by washing a handful of pearl barley in cold water, then boiling it in 1½ quarts (18 dl) of new water until completely cooked. Allow it to stand, strain – pressing the barley well into the sieve – and cool.

A cocktail without liquor that looks good as well as tasting good is an *Avocado Ade*. One good-sized avocado, a dash of chilli sauce and one of

Worcestershire, a teaspoon of horseradish, a tablespoon of lemon juice and one of mayonnaise go into a blender with ice. (You could mix this with an eggbeater, too.) Strain and serve.

In Spain they often use gaspacho, the delicious cold soup, as a cocktail after straining it. In Iran they drink a combination of one cup each of yoghurt and cucumber juice, mixed with one cup of water and a pinch of salt. They also have hundreds of tiny shops equipped simply with a juicer and plenty of fruit. These shops will sell you instant fresh juices including pomegranate – the most delectable of all.

In a kibbutz in Israel I learned about a good fruit combination: one banana to four cups of tinned grapefruit juice whirled in a blender and chilled with ice. Try it for an after school treat for your children.

If you are feeling exceptionally lazy about making a drink for a crowd of thirty non-alcholic drinkers there is nothing like *Dump Punch*, so named because you simply open up some tins and dump them into a punch bowl. It needs one tin each of frozen orange juice, frozen lemon juice and frozen pineapple juice, two quarts (2·2 l) of ginger ale, a quart of cold water and a large block of ice. Place the ice in a punch bowl, and add the rest of the ingredients. Makes forty glasses.

Another good teetotalling drink for a crowd is *Lemonale*: cool two quarts (2·2 l) of strong tea, add the juice of six lemons, a cup of sugar and several fresh mint sprigs. Just before serving pour in a quart (12 dl) of ginger ale and serve in glasses decorated with another sprig of mint.

Or how about *Mock Champagne* made of half a pint (3 dl) fresh or bottled grape juice and one-eighth of a pint (0·75 dl) orange juice to which you add a syrup made by boiling for three minutes, a quarter-pint (1·5 dl) each of sugar and water. Chill, and, just before serving add one pint (6 dl) of ginger ale.

A *Strawberry Punch* can delight young and old alike. For a children's party make three gallons (13·5 dl) by boiling four pounds (1·8 kg) of sugar in two quarts (2·2 l) of water. Cool the syrup. Combine about six pounds (2·7 kg) cleaned strawberries, eight sliced bananas, one sliced pineapple (tinned or fresh) and one pint (6 dl) mixed fruit juices, like pineapple, raspberry, currant, apple, plus the juice of twelve large oranges and twelve lemons. Add all the cooled syrup, or as much as you like, depending on the sweetness of the guests' taste. Chill all, and just before serving add four quarts (4·5 l) of soda water and as much ice as needed to make it very cold. The punch is strong but ice will thin it.

A rather professional *Lemonade* is made by using three or four table-spoons of sugar for each cup of water. Boil for two minutes to make a syrup. (This is not absolutely necessary but tastes better than when simply cold-dissolved.) Chill, and add two tablespoons of lemon juice and a pinch of salt. Ice, of course, and serve either straight or mixed with other juices or tea, to taste. A pleasant variation on this is to flavour the home-made lemonade with fresh mint as they do in Tunis.

When you are having a business lunch at home and want to remain clear headed, a *Tomato Juice Cocktail* can be whipped up that will almost replace a Bloody Mary. Take a large tin of tomato juice, two green onions with tops, the juice of one lemon, half a teaspoon of salt, a teaspoon of grated horse-radish, pepper and a dash of Tabasco. Blend together in a blender, strain and serve with ice cubes.

To accompany any meal, you can make your own *Non-Alcoholic Wine* by simply putting a bunch of grapes, seeds and all (but without stems), into your blender until they yield their juice. Sieve, and you have a delicious but slightly sweet drink.

A Capital Tea

Spiced Tea, Angostura Tea,
Iced Apple Tea, Kirsch Tea,
    Rum Highball, B and B Cream Tea,
Scotch McTavish, Alcoholic Iced Tea,
    Non-Alcoholic Iced Tea

There is early morning tea, sharp and shocking, morning tea for making a mess in the office, tea-time tea that is a social occasion, soporific bed-time tea, and generally friendly tea. The tea ceremony is not an exclusively Japanese affair, every hostess has her own, and to the real connoisseur there is a special time and place to drink each type. The subliminal but important objective for the hostess in all cases, is to receive that envied compliment on her choice of blend or flavour. Even the water plays a part. The purer the water, the better the tea is supposed to taste and rumour has it that the Queen takes specially bottled Malvern water with her wherever she goes for hers.

Britons still drink more tea per person than any other people, while the West Germans pay more for their preferred tea than any of the rest of the world. North Africans go for green tea, Russians like it stewed over a samovar, Chinese like it weak and drink it instead of water and all other non-alcoholic beverages. Americans love it iced.

Some flavours tea acquires in its own right, during its growth as green leaves or during manufacture. Some has flavour added. Darjeeling has a natural aroma of muscatel, according to Richard Pigot, a London tea merchant whose firm, run by members of his family since the eighteenth century, was probably among those that supplied the tea the Americans chucked into Boston Harbour in 1773. High-grown Ceylon tea, he claims, has a 'lemony, almost rosy' taste. Assam teas taste malty and 'red' like blackcurrants, while African teas are 'bright and good for blending'.

At risk of shattering an illusion or two, I must point out that although patriotic Americans picture the Colonists tossing tea chests into Boston harbour as if they were feathers, something is wrong with the picture. The so-called Indians that gave the British tea the heave-ho were either the off-spring of giants or had CIA help. For each chest, in those days, was filled with some 400 lbs of tea, and each was lined with about 80 lbs of lead to keep the tea dry, a total of nearly 500 lbs. Even half a dozen Heroes of the Revolution would have had trouble manhandling one chest into the sea.

Tea is a mood drink according to a dedicated tea tippling lady in London who drinks nothing else. It can be light and green and made quickly with hot, rather than boiling water, as the Chinese do, or it can be powerful and black and stewed all day long, until it becomes practically a soup, thick with sugar and hot milk. In between these extremes, what ever way you like it is right.

The English version of the tea ceremony requires the water to boil, the pot to be heated before the tea is put into it, and there must be one spoonful of tea (either India or China) for each person plus one for the pot. It should not stew but be drunk immediately. For total perfection you should have with your tea a plate of very thin cress or cucumber sandwiches and these should be served to you between four-thirty and five-thirty pm at the Ritz, among all the Right People.

In England, tea's adopted home, you are never offered just tea; it is always a 'nice cuppa tea'. What happens when the tea is not nice was graphically illustrated one day soon after I first arrived on British shores. Paper-hangers were 'decorating' my house and in my innocence I offered to make them a cup of tea. However, like the rain in the plains of Spain, the tea stayed mainly in the pot. A little while later one of the men politely asked if he could brew a cup himself. The 'nice cuppa' thus produced was almost as black as coffee, half drowned in milk, and looked to me quite undrinkable!

The British reputation for being tea drinkers is in no way pandered to by the British catering trade where, above the level of the workers' 'café', you are only allowed to drink tea at 'Tea Time' with capital 'T's. Most restaurants won't serve tea with meals and waiters raise a supercilious eyebrow if a foreigner has the temerity to ask for tea with his piece of Cheddar or with his dessert.

Still, tea survives this and has its own language. For instance, Earl Grey is a flavour designation, not a brand name as I used to think, and means that it is perfumed with oil of bergamot. Lapsang Suchong, a tea of Chinese origin, another flavour, is a large-leafed tea with a tarry, smoky taste, 'like drinking extract of railway sleepers!' Other teas are perfumed variously with lemon or lime, with jasmine, with cloves and other spices. Tea picks up flavours easily, so keep it away from soap and blue cheese. But therein lies an advantage too, because you can concoct your own favourite flavour if you want to.

Each week, on every tea estate in the world, the flavour of the growing tea is subtly altered by the changing weather and the tea taster's art is in buying months ahead to provide continuity by selecting and making sure that the taste and flavour he sells does not vary.

Picking tea is a specialized and tricky job. The bud yields the finest tea but it must be picked in just the right weather conditions. The bud makes 'golden tip'. For 'Orange Pekoe' and 'Pekoe' your picker takes one leaf and a bud. ('Two leaves and a bud is excessive,' says Mr Pigot.) Pluckers go around the gardens – nice idea that it is a garden, not a farm – every five days or so. The leaves you drink start fresh and green, but are first withered in the sun, then rolled by machine and put through a process of 'firing' which turns them black. Green tea keeps a rolled natural leaf shape.

The treated tea leaves are sorted into different grades and packed into chests for shipment. Quality depends on how tea is handled as much as anything, plus taste. Top quality is 'tip' or 'bud', running through 'pekoe' (an old Chinese name for a size of leaf), to dust. 'Fannings' are the broken-up pieces of leaf, and some tea fanciers think that the best tea is made from these fine fragments. 'The smaller the leaf the stronger the brew', because each bit contributes all of its aroma and flavour to the brew. Always make tea too strong. You can dilute it but you cannot strengthen it once brewed.

Tastes of tea that seem most popular, apart from plain India or China tea include mint – lovely either hot or cold and great for a blistering summer day. *Spiced Tea* with orange peel and cloves – a nice 'daytime tea' – is especially good with honey or brown sugar, or even with rum, on a wintry afternoon. Freshly made tea with a few fragrant rose petals dropped into each hot cup and a dash of angostura is great as a pick-me-up. Equal measures of tea and unsweetened apple juice over ice in a tall glass makes a good long drink, with a teaspoon of sugar or honey and another of fresh lemon juice.

Kirsch Tea is a rather spectacular and delicious drink to warm the cockles of your heart – if they need warming. Over three level tablespoons of sugar, in a warmed bowl, pour half a pint of kirsch and flame it for a moment or two. Quench this fire by slowly adding a half pint (3 dl) of hot black tea.

A *Rum Highball* is a simple and refreshing cool drink. Just make some good strong tea, cool it and pour into tumblers in which you have put ice and a couple of jiggers of your favourite rum. Add sugar to taste. A slice of lemon and a sprig of mint makes this a very pretty luncheon drink.

If you love Irish Coffee but can't take the caffeine, then try a *Brandy and Benedictine Cream Tea* instead: for each serving pour six ounces (175 g) freshly brewed tea into a warmed stemmed glass. Add a jigger of B & B liqueur. Do not stir but top with lightly whipped cream and sip through the cream. If, however, it's the cream that doesn't agree with you then have a

Scotch McTavish: pour a cup of boiling water over a teabag, then cover and let stand for five minutes. Remove the teabag and add a quarter of a cup of scotch whisky and a tablespoon of honey. Stir and serve.

You can make a good *Alcholic Iced Tea* for ten to twelve people by pouring a quart (2·2 l) of boiling water over twelve teabags; cover and allow to stand for five minutes. Remove the teabags, add sugar to taste and stir to dissolve. Let cool. Then add two-thirds of a cup of lemon juice and three cups of dry white wine. Pour into a tall pitcher and add ice cubes. Garnish with lemon and orange slices and a long spiral of orange peel.

If you prefer a non-alcoholic variety, then Iced Tea straight is your drink – and I think it's the best and most refreshing that there is. Here's how to make it right: first brew some fairly strong Indian tea, as much as you think you will need for a day or two. This you allow to cool, putting it in the refrigerator if there is time. When you are ready to drink it, fill a tall glass with ice and pour in the tea. Now stick in a slice of lemon – which must be crushed in the glass – and stir in some sugar until it dissolves.

And just to show you what an all-round vegetable tea is, you can also use it to keep your rose garden healthy. Empty your teapot over the roots of your roses every day during the summer. This both keeps them moist and feeds them. Tea makes a good compost, too.

If you don't like a big breakfast, but think you need sustenance in the a.m., add a lightly beaten egg to your cup of tea before taking off for the office. Full of vitamins. Finally, tea is also a source of fluoride and tea drinkers claim their dentist bills can prove it.

Tea is something to be enjoyed whenever you feel like a cup, or need a cup, or offer a cup. The choice of taste, or blend is a very personal matter but the ways it can be made and the ways it can be drunk are legion.

Confessions of
a Coffee Drinker

Irish Coffee, Galliano Whip, Caffe Amaretto,
Black Russian, Jamaican Cow, Black Rose,
Coffee Bracer, Black Jack, Café Brulot,
Café Mazagran, Coffee Grog,
Coffee Vodka, Iced Coffee

My affair with coffee, as is the case with most affairs, is a very subjective one. So my answer to the question as to which is the 'best' coffee is hugely personal. Do you like it three-quarters milk, as supplied by British Rail's station cafés; or thick and sweet as the Turks do; thin and dishwatery as in the USA; or super-concentrated, super-black with the effect of a sledgehammer, à l'Italienne? Since I enjoy variety, my tendency is to sip whatever local brews come my way, but to concentrate on the 'strong' which some experts claim is less stimulating than the 'weaker' stuff because high roasting reduces the 'stimulant ingredient', or caffeine.

Coffee prices have been skyrocketing which makes experimentation costly. Still, there are marvellous permutations of blends, roasts and brewing methods to try. I have cut my consumption of coffee by a third just so I can keep on tasting and trying different mixtures. One trick – since I do not take the time to grind my own every morning (still the best way to do it) – is to buy fresh-ground coffee and freeze it until it's needed, taking only a couple of days' supply out as required. Freezing holds in the aroma remarkably.

If you are lucky enough to have a roasting shop near you, get the merchant to give you a blend of your own. This can range from American light (ugh) to French dark or Italian espresso (aha). How fine you have it ground will depend on your method of brewing, and your coffee merchant can advise you about the grind that is best for your system. A good blend is half Mocha, half Java. Mocha is the coffee the Arabs first used, oily, heavy, with an aggressive aroma, mainly grown in the Middle East. In Germany, even today, if you want the best coffee you ask for a 'mokka'. Java is a Far Eastern coffee, light and delicate, a perfect match with Mocha.

Brazilian Santos mixed with Colombian Medellín and Venezuelan Maracaibo blends strength and subtlety. Mexico produces a rather light, mellow coffee. Indian Mysore is velvety; Sumatra has an exquisite aroma; Kenyan tiny Peaberry beans are prized. But one of the most popular coffees with connoisseurs is Jamaican Blue Mountain, among the strongest and darkest, lovely by itself if you can find it. So called Blue Mountain now often comes from Kenya because the real thing is so rare and so expensive. It is less potent but still a good variety. The thing is to try different blends yourself until you find the mix that appeals to your palate.

Best is to buy whole coffee beans, unroasted. This way they will keep almost indefinitely (only after roasting do they begin to lose flavour) and roast them yourself, blended to your individual taste.

As for the making, one rule says you should never boil coffee, but like so many rules, this one too can be broken. Old-time coffee experts say that boiling coffee is not only the easiest but best – if slightly wasteful – way to make coffee and the Turks do it all the time.

A special coffee maker with filter and plunger gives you a trouble-free boiled brew. But percolators are perhaps the most popular western way of making coffee. The filter paper method is said to be the most hygienic but my own favourite is a home espresso outfit which forces the water up through fine ground coffee by steam pressure. Makes it good and strong. Excellent after-dinner drinking.

Most coffee lovers have their quirks. I once knew a man who liked to munch roasted coffee beans in the cinema, like popcorn. At one shop I frequent a woman asked the proprietor for a mixture of all the types of coffee he had in his shop and started a whole new blend trend. Ever since he has been putting over-runs of his roastings into one big tin and calling this his Number 12 Blend. 'Even countesses come and ask for it now,' says the astonished inventor.

Coffee has been recognized as a stimulant since the ninth century when the Mullah Shadli of Aden heard that goats eating the berries of a certain bush were kept up all night as a result. Needing to keep himself alert for prayers, the Mullah brewed a beverage from them, that not only kept him widely awake but sharpened his thinking.

In its early days the Arabs used coffee as an antiseptic to wash wounds. One sultan banned it because he believed it stimulated too much thinking amongst his *hoi polloi*. Coffee drinking was punished by beating. Thinking was punished by death!

The news of coffee's stimulating qualities spread around Arabia and eventually to Europe where the 'café' has become the rallying point for intellectuals and literati of all sorts. Some whose inspiration was enhanced thus were Voltaire, Rousseau, Pope, Swift, Nietzsche, Thomas Mann, Mendelssohn, J. S. Bach who even composed a 'Cantata to Coffee', Oscar Wilde, Byron, Casanova who drank it as a revivifyer after a particularly exhausting conquest, and Camus who wrestled with Existentialism in Paris's Café Flore.

In addition to simply drinking coffee straight, some agreeably alcoholic variations exist. Everyone knows what the Irish have done to improve the brew – they top up black coffee, after sugaring it to taste, with a healthy measure of Irish whiskey and a dollop of thick cream. The Italians have jumped in with a half pint (3 dl) of double cream whipped with two ounces (50 ml) of Galliano floating on a cup of coffee. And *Amaretto*, combined in equal quantities with rum in coffee is another happy Italian contribution.

Some liqueurs are made with coffee. One is Tia Maria, not only delicious by itself but if mixed (one part) with two parts of vodka giving you a *Black Russian*. Blending a third of coffee liqueur with two-thirds of milk produces a healthy beverage with a kick, called a *Jamaican Cow*. Other coffee liqueurs you may like include Mexican Kahlua, Italian Expresso, German Kirsch mit Mokka.

The Danes clarify their coffee interestingly. They place a small silver coin in a coffee cup and pour hot coffee over it until the coin becomes invisible. Then they pour aquavit in until it appears again, whereupon the drink is ready for internal application. A dash of cognac in after-dinner coffee is also a good idea.

For a *Black Rose*, which is another good after-dinner drink, you need a measure of light rum in a tumbler, two ice cubes, a teaspoon of sugar and cold black coffee. For a *Coffee Bracer*, fill a tall glass with crushed ice and strong coffee, top with demerara rum, add sugar and cream to taste, garnish with a pinch of powdered cloves or allspice and stir with a cinnamon stick if you have one. A *Black Jack* is made from two ounces (50 ml) of Black Jack brandy and an ounce (25 ml) each of kirsch and black coffee frappéed in fine ice.

At the risk of being accused of thinking too much, a l'Arabe, you might try impressing your guests with *Café Brulot*. You need a chafing dish for this black magic ceremony. Place in it five or six zests of orange, three or four of lemon, two sticks of broken cinnamon bark, ten headless cloves, eight lumps of sugar, and two coffee cups of cognac. Light the burner, stir the mixture until warm, then set it alight. Allow it to burn a minute then pour in five coffee cupfuls of double-strength black coffee, ladle into coffee cups for drinking. Most impressive in a darkened room. An easier coffee drink is *Café Mazagran* – double strength coffee and red wine in equal quantities served hot and sweetened to taste.

To make *Coffee Grog*, pack crushed ice into a tall glass and pour on very strong coffee, add sugar and cream as you would for hot coffee, then a measure of dark rum. Garnish with a pinch each of clove, allspice and cinnamon if you want to. For *Coffee Vodka*, take four cups each of vodka, water and sugar, and a half pound (225 g) of freshly ground coffee. Pour one cup of vodka over the coffee grounds and let that steep for a week. Make a syrup of the sugar and water and the three remaining cups of vodka, combine this with the coffee and vodka. Strain, bottle and store for six months to let the taste meld. Drink if you are Russian, sip if you are not. *Iced Coffee* is a good summer treat. Simply make strong coffee, let it cool and pour it into a tall glass with two or three ice cubes. Add cream and sugar to taste.

Finally, you can grow your own coffee, though it will hardly help your finances since it takes five years for one bush to produce three pounds of beans. Meantime, however, it is lovely to look at with its waxy flowers, shiny green leaves, and fat berries that turn yellow and then red as they ripen and have, as you'd expect, a sensational aroma.

Index

Abdug, 42
Advocaat Lemonade, 116
alcohol, white, how to make, 64–5
Alcoholic Iced Tea, 151
ale, see Champagne Punch
Alexander, 23
Alexander's Sister, 60
Almond Blossom, 52
American Rose, 52
Angostura Highball, 142
Angostura Ice Cubes, 64, 115
Angostura Tea, 150
aperitifs, 13–18
Apple Punch, 144
applejack, how to make, 51, 136
aquavit, in coffee, 156; see also Danish Mary
Arco-Iris, 52
Avocado Ade, 144–5

B and B Cream Tea, 150
Bamboo, 74
Barking Dog, 24
Barley Water, 144
Bathtub Vodka, 45
beef bouillon, see Bullshot, Cowshot
beer, see recipes in BEER 129–34; see also Dog's Nose
Beetroot Savoury, 127
Benedictine, see Mule's Hind Leg
Bergamot Tea, 32
Black Cossack, 46
Black Cow, 144
Black Jack, 156
Black Rose, 39, 156
Black Russian, 59, 156
Black Velvet, 87
Bloodshot, 46
Bloody Mary, 18, 45
Bob's Bloody Mary, 45–6
Brandied Duck, 54
Brandied Fruit, 54–5
brandy (see also cognac), in cooking, 52–5; fine à l'eau, 61; see recipes in COGNAC

47–55; see also Chilled Champagne Cocktail, Connoisseur's Milk Punch, Egg Nog, Elk, Four-Man Cider Cup, Green Beret Basque, Hop Toad, Kirsch Tea, Mule's Hind Leg, Orange Brulot, Personal Punch, Ruby Punch, Sundowner
Brandy Balls, 54
Brandy Mayonnaise, 53
Brandy Scaffa, 52
Brandy Sling, 52
Brandy Vinaigrette, 53
Bronx, 23
Broodje, 133
Bulldog, 24
Bullshot, 46
Burgundy Cup, 102
Buttered Rum, 131
Buttered Whisky, 121

Café Brulot, 156
Café Calypso, 59
Café Mazagran, 156
Caffe Amaretto, 156
Calisay, 24
calvados, 51, 121
Calvados Cup, 138
Campari, 15; see also Red Lips
Cannonball, 116
Caramel Carrots, 28
Carp in Beer, 133
Cat's Eye, 24
champagne, see recipes in CHAMPAGNE 81–9; see also American Rose, Bergamot Tea, Champagne Cassis, Extra Festive Champagne Punch
Champagne Cassis, 14
Champagne Punch, 86
Chantecleer, 24
Chartreuse, green, see Arco-Iris, Green Dragon, Green Eyed Monster
Chartreuse Mix, 60
Chartreuse, yellow, see Arco-Iris, Yellow Parrot

Cheese and Brandy Dip, 53
Cherry Heering, with tequila, 114; see also Heering Fizz
Chicken with Cider Sauce, 137–8
Chilled Champagne Cocktail, 86
Chilled Elderflower, 143–4
chilli peppers, in sherry, 72; in vodka, 18
Chinese Herb Highball, 63
Chocolate Malted Milk, 144
Christmas Terrine, 124
Chufa, 143
cider, in cooking, 137–8, 140; see recipes in CIDER 135–40; see also Apple Punch, Buttered Rum
Cider Apple Sauce, 140
Cider Punches, 138, 139–40
Cider Soup, 140
Cider Sparkle, 138
Cinzano, 15
Citron Pressé, 143
clam juice, see Bullshot
Clam Juice Cocktail, 142
coffee, see recipes in COFFEE 153–7; see also Café Calypso, Coffee Cocktail, Marnissimo, Mexican Coffee
Coffee Bracer, 156
Coffee Cocktail, 18
Coffee Grog, 156–7
Coffee Vodka, 44, 157
cognac, as aperitif, 16; in peach brandy, 62; see recipes in COGNAC 47–55; see also Alexander's Sister, Black Jack, Café Brulot, Champagne Punch, Chartreuse Mix, Chinese Herb Highball, Coffee Cocktail, Egg Nog, Green Dragon, La Rose Americaine, Modern Grog, Mulled Wine, Side Car, Stirrup Cup
cointreau, see Coffee Cocktail, Malt Side Car, Side Car

cola, *see* Black Cow, Cuba Libre, Portcola
Connoisseur's Milk Punch, 122
Cooch Behar, 46
coolers, 116
Corn Popper, 32
Cowshot, 73
cream, *see* Corn Popper, Cream Punch, Frozen Alexander's Sister, Galliano, Grasshopper, Irish Coffee, Marnissimo, White Shoulders
Cream Punch, 33
crème de cacao, *see* Arco-Iris, Alexander, Coffee Cocktail, Grasshopper
crème de menthe, frappé, 18; *see also* Alexander's Sister, Grasshopper, Green Dragon, Secret, White Scorpion
crème de violettes, *see* Orchid
Crow, 32
Cuba Libre, 39
curaçao, *see* Champagne Punch, Euphoria, Modern Grog, Ruby Punch, Sundowner, White Shoulders

Daiquiri, 39
Danish Beer Soup, 133
Danish Mary, 66
Devil, 80
Dog's Nose, 24
Dragoon Punch, 87
Drambuie, with strawberries, 62
Dry Manhattan, 15, 31
Dry Martini, 22
Dubonnet, as aperitif, 15; frappé, 18
Dubonnet Orange Fizz, 115; *see also* Orange Fizz, Pink Fizz, Whisky Fizz
Dubonnet Whisky Fizz, 115
Dump Punch, 145

Egg Nog, 121–2
Eggs, in tea, 151; *see also* Chilled Elderflower, Egg Nog, Connoisseur's Milk Punch, Port Flip, Prairie Chicken, Punch-à-Crème,

Sherry Flip, Sherry Puff
Elk, 24
Euphoria, 113
Extra Festive Champagne Punch, 123–4

Fishhouse Punch, 39
Four-Man Cider Cup, 139
Franco-Russian Cocktail, 44
Frappés, 18
French Kir, 18
Frozen Alexander's Sister, 60

Galliano, *see* Galliano Whip, Wallbanger
Galliano Whip, 156
Gelée aux Xeres, 73
German Bowle, 86
Gibson, 22
gin, *see* recipes in GIN 19–24; *see also* Alexander's Sister, Almond Blossom, Angostura Highball, Cider Sparkle, Green Dragon, Green Eyed Monster, Hintlesham White Lady, Mint Magic, Orange Fizz, Orchid, Pink Gin, Pink Lime, Singapore Gin Sling, Spanish Rosita, Straight Law, White Lady
Gin and Lime, 23
ginger ale, *see* Angostura Highball, Bulldog, Chinese Herb Highball, Dump Punch, Highland Cooler, Lemonale, Mock Champagne, Redcurrant Cooler
ginger beer, *see* Moscow Mule
Gluhwein, 121
Golnar, 114
Grand Gimlet, 45
Grand Marnier, *see* Marnissimo
grape juice, *see* Mock Champagne
grapefruit juice, Pernod and, 15; *see also* Euphoria, Kibbutz Fruit Cocktail, MJP, Moscow Mule
Grasshopper, 60
Green Beret Basque, 64
Green Dragon, 60–61

Green Eyed Monster, 52
Green Izarra Jelly, 60
Green Knight, 74
Green Treetop, 44
grenadine, *see* La Rose Americaine, In-Drink
Guinness, *see* Black Cossack, Stout Cocktail

Ham baked in Cider, 137
hangover, remedies for: champagne, 87; consommé with sherry, 73; Fernet-Branca, 15; Mongole Soup, 75
Heering Fizz, 59
hiccoughs, remedy for, 17
Highland Cooler, 31
Hintlesham White Lady, 18
Hippocras, 64
Home-made Beer, 130
Home-made Peach Liqueur, 62
Hop Toad, 117

ice cream *see* Black Cow, Chocolate Malted Milk, Silver Stallion
Iced Coffee, 157
Iced Apple Tea, 150
In-Drink, 116
Iranian Yoghurt Cocktail, 145
Irish Coffee, 156
Irish Fizz, 33
Italian Manhattan, 51
Izarra, *see* Arco-Iris, Green Beret Basque, Green Izarra Jelly

Jamaican Cow, 156
John Collins, 21

Kalte Ente, 125
Karkade, 143
Kibbutz Fruit Cocktail, 145
Kir, 102
Kirsch Tea, 150
Kirschwasser, 24
Kojak, 33

La Rose Americaine, 115
Lebanese Cinnamon Tea, 144
Leek Soup, 75

lemon juice, *see* Bloodshot, Brandy Sling, Champagne Punch, Chantecleer, Chartreuse Mix, Chinese Herb Highball, Cider Punch, Cider Sparkle, Crow, Cuba Libre, Dump Punch, Fishhouse Punch, Green Treetop, Heering Fizz, Highland Cooler, Hintlesham White Lady, Hop Toad, Lemon Punch, Lemonade, Malt Side Car, Orange Fizz, Personal Punch Framboise, Pink Elephant, Ramos Fizz, Rattlesnake, Ruby Punch, Silver Stallion, Singapore Gin Sling, Stirrup Cup, Strawberry Punch, Sundowner, Tomato Cocktail, Treetop, Tunisian Freshener, White Lady
Lemon Punch, 86–7
Lemon Vodka, 44
lemonade, *see* Advocaat Lemonade, Cat's Eye, Lemonade, Port and Lemon Cooler
Lemonade, 146
Lemonale, 145
lime juice, *see* Daiquiri, Gin and Lime, Grand Gimlet, Green Knight, Marie Galante, Mona's Rum Punch, Moscow Mule, Orange Fizz, Pink Lime, Zombie
liqueurs, *see* recipes in LIQUEURS 58–67
Lobster au Cognac, 54

Malt Rob Roy, 31
Malt Side Car, 31
maraschino, *see* Brandy Scaffa, Champagne Punch, Four-Men Cider Cup, Rhine Wine Punch
Marie Galante, 39
Marnissimo, 61
Martini, 15
Mexican Coffee, 142
Mexican Peter, 114
milk, *see* Chilled Elderflower, Chocolate Malted Milk,

Egg Nog, Jamaican Cow, Connoiseur's Milk Punch, Port Nightcap, Rum Cow, Mint Julep, 32–3
Mint Magic, 18
MJP, 39
Mock Champagne, 145
Modern Grog, 38
Mona's Rum Punch, 38
Mongole Soup, 75
Moscow Mule, 46
Mule's Hind Leg, 24
Mulled Cider, 139
Mulled Wine, 120–21

Negus, 80
non-alcoholic drinks, *see* recipes in NON-ALCOHOLIC DRINKS 141–6
Non-Alcoholic Iced Tea, 151
Non-Alcoholic Wine, 146

Old Fashioned, 33
Old Pepper, 32
Orange Brulot, 122–3
Orange Fizz, 115
orange juice, ouzo or Pernod with, 15; *see also* Apple Punch, Bulldog, Buttered Whisky, Champagne Punch, Cider Punch, Dubonnet Fizz, Dump Punch, In-Drink, Orange Fizz, Ruby Punch, Screwdriver, Sherry with Orange, Strawberry Punch, Sundowner, Wallbanger
Orchid, 52
ouzo, 15
Ouzo with Vermouth, 15

Palmer, 32
papaya juice, *see* Zombie
Paradise, 139
passion fruit juice, *see* Kojak
Peach Liqueur, Home-made, 62
pepper, Italian or Mexican, *see* Cooch Behar
Pernod, frappé, 18; with fruit juice, 15; with vermouth, 15; *see also* Perroquet, Yellow Parrot
Perroquet, 114
Personal Punch Framboise, 87

pineapple juice, *see* Euphoria, Zombie
Pink Elephant, 33
Pink Fizz, 115
Pink Gin, 17
Pink Lime, 17
Pink Vodka, 44
Planter's Punch, 39
Polish Bigos, 124
pomegranate juice, *see* Golnar, port, as aperitif, 16; *see* recipes in PORT, 77–80; *see also* Cannonball, Egg Nog
Port Cocktail, 80
Port Flip, 80
Port and Lemon Cooler, 79
Port and Orange Cooler, 79
Port Nightcap, 80
Port Royal, 39
Port and Soda, 80
Portcola, 79
Porter, *see* Dragoon Punch
Prairie Chicken, 24
Prohibition Cocktail, 22
punches, *see* Apple Punch, Champagne Punch, Cider Punches, Connoisseur's Milk Punch, Corn Popper, Cream Punch, Dragoon Punch, Dump Punch, Euphoria, Extra Festive Champagne Punch, Fishhouse Punch, Lemon Punch, Mona's Rum Punch, Personal Punch Framboise, Planter's Punch, Punch-à-Crème, Random Punch, Redcurrant Punch, Rhine Wine Punch, Ruby Punch, Rum Punch, Strawberry Punch
Punch-à-Crème, 37
Punt e Mes, 15

Ramos Fizz, 23
Random Punch, 86
Rasputin, 46
Rattlesnake, 32
Red Lips, 46
Red-Hot Aperitif, 17–18
Redcurrant Cooler, 142–3
Redcurrant Punch, 142
Reform, 74
Revolution, 79
Rhine Wine Punch, 102

Rose Water, 64
Rossi, 15
Ruby Punch, 102
rum, *see* recipes in RUM 35–9;
   see also Buttered Rum,
   Café Calypso, Caffe
   Amaretto, Coffee Bracer,
   Coffee Grog, Egg Nog,
   Un Grog, Zombie
Rum Cow, 39
Rum Highball, 150
Rum Pot, 39
Rum Punch, 37, 38
Russo-Spanish Cocktail, 44

St Raphael with Holland
   gin, 23
Sangria, 115
Sauerkraut in Beer, 134
Scandinavian Cherry Dip, 59
Scotch Bonnet, 72–3
Scotch McTavish, 151
Screwdriver, 45, 59
Secret, 31
Serpent's Tooth, 32
sherry, in cooking, 72–3, 75;
   with orange juice, 116;
   with tonic water, 16;
   see recipes in SHERRY 69–
   75; *see also* Cannonball,
   Egg Nog, Vodkatini
Sherry Flip, 74
Sherry with Orange, 74
Sherry Puff, 73
Ship, 74
Side Car, 18
Silver Stallion, 24
Singapore Gin Sling, 112
sloe gin, 21
Sol y Sombra, 52
Solid Pink Gin, 23
Sorbet aux Framboises, 62
Spanish Rosita, 52
Spiced Cider, 138
Spiced Tea, 150
Steamed Haggis, 29
Stirrup Cup, 123
stout, *see* Black Velvet,
   Dog's Nose, Stout
   Cocktail
Stout Cocktail, 32
Straight Law, 74
Strawberry Punch, 145–6
Sundowner, 113

Tarragon Vodka, 44

tea, *see* recipes in TEA 147–
   51; *see also* Bergamot Tea,
   Lemonale, Modern Grog,
   Mulled Cider, Rhine
   Wine Punch, Tea à la
   Russe
Tea à la Russe, 113
tequila, *see* In-Drink,
   Mexican Peter
Tia Maria, *see* Black Russian,
   Café Calypso, Port Royal
Tipsy Cake, 73
Tom Collins, 21
Tomato Cocktail, 146
tomato juice, *see* Bloody
   Mary, Cooch Behar,
   Danish Mary, Tomato
   Cocktail
Treetop, 23
Triple Sec, *see* Marie
   Galante
Tunisian Freshener, 146

Un Grog, 123

Van der Hum, *see* Sundowner
vermouth, aperitifs, 15;
   with cassis, 18; frappé, 18;
   see also Bamboo, Barking
   Dog, Bronx, Cat's Eye,
   Devil, Dry Manhattan,
   Dry Martini, Gibson,
   Green Eyed Monster,
   Green Knight, Italian
   Manhattan, Malt Rob Roy,
   Spanish Rosita, Vodkatini
vodka, encased in ice,
   42; to flavour, 43–4;
   see recipes in VODKA 41–6;
   see also Angostura High-
   ball, Black Russian, Golnar,
   Green Dragon, Red-Hot
   Aperitif, Revolution,
   Screwdriver, Wallbanger,
   White Scorpion
Vodkatini, 44

Wallbanger, 59
whisky, *see* recipes in
   WHISKY 25–33; *see also*
   Buttered Whisky, Dry
   Manhattan, Dubonnet
   Whisky Fizz, Egg Nog,
   Irish Coffee, Scotch
   McTavish, Ship
Whisky Sour, 31

White Lady, 18
White Scorpion, 24
White Shoulders, 46
wine, as aperitif, 16; cassis
   with, 18; raspberry brandy
   with, 51; *see* recipes in WINE
   91–102; *see also* Alcoholic
   Iced Tea, Café Mazagran,
   Egg Nog, Gluhwein,
   Hippocras, Kalte Ente, Kir,
   Mint Magic, Mulled
   Wine, Sangria, Stout
   Cocktail
wine, cooling, 106; decanting,
   106; effect of age on, 107–8;
   storing, 105, 107; tasting,
   104–5
wines, sparkling, 87–9
Winter Mull, 138

Yellow Parrot, 116
yoghurt, *see* Abdug, Iranian
   Yoghurt Cocktail

Zambucca, 121
Zombie, 116–17

ST. VINCENT
PATRON SAINT OF WINE